Robert Burns

Twayne's English Authors Series

Herbert Sussman, Editor

Northeastern University

TEAS 452

ROBERT BURNS
1759–1796
Reprinted with the permission of
the National Portrait Gallery, London

Robert Burns

By Raymond Bentman

Temple University

Twayne Publishers
A Division of G. K. Hall & Co. • *Boston*

For Katharine and Leslie

Copyediting supervised by Lewis DeSimone
Book production by Janet Zietowski
Book design by Barbara Anderson

Typeset in 11 pt. Garamond
by Compset, Inc., of Beverly, Massachusetts

Printed on permanent/durable acid-free paper
and bound in the United States of America

Library of Congress Cataloging in Publication Data

Bentman, Raymond.
  Robert Burns.

  (Twayne's English authors series ; TEAS 452)
  Bibliography: p.
  Includes index.
  1. Burns, Robert, 1759–1796—Criticism and
interpretation.   I. Title.   II. Series.
PR4338.B46   1987   821'.6   87-8554
ISBN 0-8057-6952-8 (alk. paper)

Contents

About the Author
Preface
Chronology

> *Chapter One*
> The Background and Early Years   1

> *Chapter Two*
> The Satiric and Moral Poetry   20

> *Chapter Three*
> The Songs   69

> *Chapter Four*
> Burns and the Late Eighteenth Century   104

> *Chapter Five*
> Conclusion   139

Notes and References   141
Selected Bibliography   148
Index   152

About the Author

Raymond Bentman received his B.A. from Kenyon College and his Ph.D. from Yale University. He is a professor of English at Temple University and has previously taught at the University of Michigan.

Raymond Bentman's essays on Burns have appeared in *University of Texas Studies in Literature and Language, From Sensibility to Romanticism,* edited by Frederick Hilles and Harold Bloom, *Studies in Romanticism,* and *The Wordsworth Circle.* He is the editor of the Cambridge Editions volume of Robert Burns. He has also published on Greek literature and on Swift and is the editor of the Augustan Reprint Society edition of *The Methodist,* by Evan Lloyd.

Preface

Since this book is an introduction to Burns's work, I have under-
taken to make it informational and objective. But I have a thesis: Burns
is the first poet to treat, in the context of concrete experience, those
subjects that have come to inspire and haunt the modern world: equality of all people; the delights and dangers of personal freedom outside
the restraints of church and state; the wonders and bewilderment of
making one's own way without the guidance of traditions or religious
principles; the value of emotions; and the uncertainty of all knowledge.
He lived out these ideas, and he translated them into a new idiom, one
that he created out of his ability to merge the English with the Scottish
literary traditions, to reconcile formal poetry with the folk song, and
to integrate the ideas of the Enlightenment with his experience as a
farmer.

The first chapter gives some of the intellectual, literary, and historical background that is essential for understanding a poet who was
strongly influenced by his time and who used the traditions so crea-
tively. The second and third chapters sketch his life in relation to his
poetry, for the way he lived and what he wrote are integrally associated.
In his early career he wrote in a satiric tradition, combining the styles
of English Augustan poetry and eighteenth-century Scottish literature
and folk song. But even in the early poetry, written mostly in 1785,
he started moving away from satire toward a poetry that was less prescriptive and more receptive to human limitations. Later in his career
he turned to songwriting, concentrating on the expression of emotions.
This movement, from ethical poetry to emotional poetry, while strikingly independent, was consonant with much of the writing of the late
eighteenth century. For this reason the last chapter examines Burns as
a writer of his age in Britain. His poetry can best be understood and
enjoyed when seen as an expression of his own conflicts and of the
conflicts of the restless, experimental, revolutionary age he lived in.

Burns is one of the great British poets of the eighteenth century,
but for various reasons he has often been underrated or ignored. The
superficial difficulty of his vocabulary is one. Another reason is that his
exceptional originality makes his style difficult to categorize. And an-

other problem is that the late eighteenth century itself is difficult to define. Scholars and critics have far too often resolved these various problems by ignoring Burns or by hiding him in some out-of-the-way niche. In doing so they have missed much that both Burns and the age have to say.

Recently, scholarship has begun to show greater respect for the late eighteenth century and for Burns's place in it. Several important books and essays examine the late eighteenth century and reveal that its marvelous volatility is an appropriate metaphor for a literature that confronts the sensibilities of the modern age. Fredric V. Bogel's *Literature and Insubstantiality* is a suggestive examination of some of the important trends of the age. Carol McGuirk's *Robert Burns and the Sentimental Era* is the best book so far to treat Burns as a poet of his own age in Britain.

Bogel has strongly influenced my view of the period, and McGuirk has influenced my view of Burns's place in it. Indeed, I would bore the reader and embarrass the authors were I to give them all the credit that is their due. I have, therefore, limited myself to an occasional quotation from their books, but I owe them more. I also owe a great deal, as does anyone who works with Burns, to James Kinsley's edition of Burns's works, especially to the notes, with their wealth of information and critical observations. And David Daiches's *Robert Burns* remains, thirty-six years after its publication, still a source of useful information and fresh insight.

My thanks are due to many people and institutions. Among them, I am especially grateful to the students in my graduate seminar on the late eighteenth century that I taught in fall 1985. The students in that wonderful class provided me with a constant source of new observations on the period and acted as a regular sounding board for my ideas, especially those in the last chapter of this book. My thanks are also due to Temple University for granting me a study leave and for the staff of Paley library, in particular Rosamond Putzel. I want to thank Vittorio Ginzburg and Marilyn Gaull for their patient and assiduous reading of the manuscript in its various stages and Carol McGuirk for a useful, stimulating correspondence. And I especially want to thank my colleague and friend, Richard Beckman, for innumerable stimulating conversations about Burns, the age, and the nature of poetry. I must thank him in particular for his reading of the manuscript. If errors and foolishness remain, they will not exist for any lack of his concern, thoroughness, or relentless critical acumen.

Raymond Bentman

Temple University

Chronology

1759   Robert Burns born 25 January in Alloway, Scotland

1765   With his brother, Gilbert, begins schooling under John Murdoch.

1766   The family moves to Mount Oliphant, a farm two miles from Alloway, where life is very hard. They will stay there for eleven years.

1768   Murdoch leaves Alloway. Their father takes up the boys' education.

1772   Goes on alternate weeks to Dalrymple School.

1773   Studies with Murdoch for three weeks. Revises his grammar and learns French.

1774   Writes his first poem, a song called "O once I lov'd."

1777   The family moves to Lochlie Farm where life is less hard. Reading increases.

1779   Goes to dancing school against his father's wishes.

1780   The Tarbolton Bachelors' Club is founded.

1781   Works as a flax-dresser in Irvine. Meets Richard Brown.

1783   Begins the *First Commonplace Book*. Robert and Gilbert rent Mossgiel farm.

1784   Father dies. The family moves to Mossgiel.

1785   Betty Paton bears Burns a daughter, Elizabeth. Meets Jean Armour and begins to write major poetry. By the end of the year has written most of the poetry that will appear in the Kilmarnock Edition.

1786   Plans to emigrate to Jamaica. Proposal for the Kilmarnock Edition is sent to the publishers in April. James Armour repudiates Burns as Jean Armour's husband in late April. In July does penance for fornication. In late July *Poems* are published at Kilmarnock. In September Jean bears him twins. In November leaves for Edinburgh. In December the Edinburgh Edition is announced.

1787   The Edinburgh Edition is published in April. Tours the Border Country and the Highlands. Begins to work with Johnson on *The Scots Musical Museum*. Back in Edinburgh meets Agnes M'Lehose (Clarinda).

1788   Begins to visit Clarinda in Edinburgh. Visits Jean Armour in Mauchline. In April acknowledges Jean as his wife. Settles on a farm in Ellisland. In July receives excise commission. Becomes virtual editor of *Scots Musical Museum* and a regular contributor of songs.

1789   Begins his excise duties.

1790   Writes *Tam o'Shanter*.

1791   Gives up farm at Ellisland and moves to Dumfries in order to work full time in the excise. *Tam o'Shanter* is published.

1792   Agrees to contribute to Thomson's *Select Collection*.

1793   The second Edinburgh edition is published. Makes substantial contributions to *Select Collection*.

1795   Becomes severely ill in December.

1796   Dies at Dumfries on 21 July.

Chapter One

The Background and Early Years

Burns's Early Years

Robert Burns was born in 1759 in Ayrshire, a rural area of southwest Scotland, and lived most of his life on farms, in villages, or in small towns in the same county. He lived with his family in virtual isolation on a small, impoverished farm during some of his most formative years. His education consisted mostly of self-education and a few, scattered years with a local schoolmaster. Out of this extremely unpromising background came one of the most important British poets of the eighteenth century. Obviously his inborn genius was the most significant factor in bringing about this unlikely phenomenon. But his position in life, his nationality and religion, and the state of the world all worked together to make him the particular kind of poet he was.

His life spans the second half of the eighteenth century, a period of extraordinary change in British, European, and American politics, religion, philosophy, and aesthetics. The great influences on his poetry, however, were not just the obvious, dramatic changes—the French and American revolutions, the Industrial Revolution—but also the subtler, less easily defined philosophical, religious, nationalistic, and literary changes that were present everywhere in this volatile half century.

Several influences helped to shape his personality and give direction to his creative ability: his father and home life generally; Presbyterianism, the powerful and pervasive church of Scotland; his unconventional but good education; the literary and intellectual milieu of late eighteenth-century Britain; and Scottish nationalism and the Scottish Revival in literature.

When Burns was born, his father, William Burnes (the spelling was changed later), was employed as a gardener in Alloway, Ayrshire. He was determined to improve his situation by becoming a tenant farmer, so in 1766, when Burns was seven, his father rented a farm at Mount

1

Oliphant, near Alloway. The move was financially a mistake, and the family had to struggle for eleven years, living in extreme poverty and isolation, while laboring constantly. Burns describes his experience of those years as the "chearless gloom of a hermit with the unceasing moil of a galley-slave."[1] His father did everything in his power to make the farm successful, but he was the victim of bad luck, unfortunate timing, and perhaps mistaken judgment.

The comments on his father's character are universally favorable. He was a stern and upright man, but fair and genuinely desirous to have the best for his children. There seems to have been, however, some personality conflict between Burns and his father. William Burnes was a relatively liberal man for his time, but he was old-fashioned in his ideas of proper behavior and a man of strong opinion, "the sport of strong passions" (R 125), as Burns says. And Burns, while an essentially obedient young man, had a wild streak in him, or perhaps what he himself called a "stubborn, sturdy something in my disposition."

One of the few firm details we have of their conflict involves Burns's desire to attend dancing school. His father opposed it, and Burns went anyway. The issue seems unimportant, the sort of conflict any strong-willed father and strong-willed young son might have. But neither regarded it as such. Burns says, several years later, "My going was, what to this hour I repent, in absolute defiance of his commands" (R 125). Burns also reports the effect on his father: "From that instance of rebellion he took a kind of dislike to me, which I believe was one cause of that dissipation which marked my future years." But then Burns does a turnabout. "I only say, Dissipation, comparative with the strictness and sobriety of Presbyterean country life; for though the will-o'-wisp meteors of thoughtless Whim were almost the sole lights of my path, yet early ingrained Piety and Virtue never failed to point me out the line of Innocence."

Burns is surely right in saying that he seemed dissipated only in comparison with the strict Presbyterian morals of a Scottish village. It is true that he fathered a few illegitimate children and enjoyed drinking with his friends. But illegitimate children were not uncommon at a time when birth control was all but unknown, and Burns always took responsibility for his children. His drinking, from all accounts, was not excessive.

The comments about the controversy over dancing school suggest that this event was merely one sign of some much larger discord. Words and phrases like "repent," "absolute defiance," "rebellion," "dislike to me," "dissipation," "thoughtless Whim," "early ingrained Piety and Virtue," and "way of Innocence" reflect a great deal of conflict with his father and within himself. That he could apply "dissipation" and "virtue" to himself in the same sentence suggests that he was never entirely at peace with either irreligious pleasure or religious restraint. That he could repent all his life over a small, youthful act of rebellion suggests that he was never able to break entirely from parental dominance. And we might guess that the terrible strains created by extreme hard work, isolation, deprivation, and constant financial worry would have seriously intensified the conflict between father and son.

Burns's personality, as shown in his writings and in descriptions of him by contemporaries, was that of a man of profoundly mixed emotions. He had a capacity for joy and pleasure that was remarkable. Few poets have expressed more eloquently the simple joys of love and sex, of friendship, of drinking, of such ordinary pleasures as eating, talking, or walking in the countryside. And the joys were genuine. But he was also subject to repeated spells of depression that started early in life and seem rarely to have left him entirely. Throughout his letters he makes such remarks about himself as, to his father in 1781, "Perhaps very soon, I shall bid an eternal adieu to all the pains, & uneasiness & disquietudes of this weary life" (R 4). He refers to himself, in 1786, as "one of the rueful-looking, long-visaged sons of Disappointment" (R 29). In his autobiographical letter (R 125) he speaks of his "miserable fog of ennui" and his "idle terrors." And he reports that these various forms of depression never leave him entirely: "Even in the hour of social mirth, my gaiety is the madness of an intoxicated criminal under the hands of the executioner" (R 53). Biographers have often portrayed him as a joyful man who suffered from intermittent periods of depression. The truth seems to be, rather, that he was a man of substantially varied emotions.

Burns's satires may result, as John Weston argues, from the anger that stemmed from "his own personal outrage and pain from social and economic injustice experienced by him and his family during the starvation years from six to eighteen at Mt. Oliphant farm."[2] He knew well that his family was the victim of a system that increasingly disfavored the tenant farmer. His writings at times express rage against the class system and the economic unfairness of his world. And they also express a deep commitment to the contrary, to the desire of controlling one's own fortunes in a world that promised independence but rarely delivered on its promise. Burns was to become one of the first and most articulate poetic exponents of democracy and individual freedom. His depression and anger provided him with a powerful impetus to pursue personal independence and to express his belief in it so eloquently.

Robert Fitzhugh suggests that Burns's depression may have been due to "religious concern, poor diet, hard work, and frustration."[3] Burns says something similar when he describes himself as "The sport, the miserable victim, of rebellious pride; hypochondriac imagination, agonizing sensibility, and bedlam passions" (R 185)! Another probable cause for his depression, then, was the serious conflict in which he lived most of his life. He tried to be a good, obedient son and also to go his own rebellious way. He wanted personal independence but could never shake off his father's control. He thought of himself as at once both dissipated and virtuous. His passions drove him to behave in ways that were contrary to his father's principles, which he was never able to dismiss, and to the morals of a church that he could never entirely abandon. His education, reading, and intellectual background also showed significant divisions, but in a way that provided him with an idiom appropriate to express some of these conflicts.

Burns's Education

Burns's education and readings consisted, on one hand, of eighteenth-century English literature, the Bible, and some of the more important older English literature; and, on the other hand, of folk tales and folk songs. And in the middle, providing a model for a synthesis of the two trends, were the works of contemporary Scotsmen, particularly Robert Fergusson.

Burns's had about two years of formal schooling, at the ages of six and seven, with John Murdoch, a schoolmaster brought in to teach the sons of the local farmers, and a few weeks' more schooling in his early teens. His father supervised his education at other times. The readings with Murdoch consisted mostly of the Bible and selections from Shakespeare, Milton, Dryden, and several popular eighteenth-century English authors. His father supplied him with theological, historical, and geographical readings. He added a considerable amount of reading on his own, so that by the time he began to write poetry he was well versed in Shakespeare and Milton and in most writers of the previous decades—Pope, Addison, Gray, Shenstone, Macpherson, Sterne, Richardson (only *Pamela*), Smollett, and Henry Mackenzie; and the philosophers Locke and Adam Smith. He refers to other English authors later in life, especially praising Goldsmith and Cowper. But he probably did not read their works in time to be influenced by them in his early poetry.

A second important influence was the folk tradition. Its influence started early. Burns reports that "In my infant and boyish days too, I owed much to an old Maid of my Mother's, remarkable for her ignorance, credulity and superstition.—She had, I suppose, the largest collection in the county of tales and songs concerning devils, ghosts, fairies, brownies, witches, warlocks, spunkies, kelpies, elf-candles, dead-lights, wraiths, apparitions, cantraips, giants, inchanted towers, dragons and other trumpery.—This cultivated the latent seeds of Poesy" (R 125). He reports that, later in his life, a "Collection of Songs was my vade mecum.—I pored over them, driving my cart or walking to labor, song by song, verse by verse; carefully noting the true tender or sublime from affection and fustian.—I am convinced I owe much to this for my critic-craft such as it is" (R 125).

A third influence on Burns was the eighteenth-century Scottish Literary Revival, in particular its writers Allan Ramsay and Robert Fergusson. This revival, along with the interest in songs, was so important for Burns, and partook of so many of the historical and intellectual forces that helped to mold Burns, that we need first to examine other aspects of the historical, religious, and intellectual background in order to place this revival, and its influence on Burns, in its proper context.

Burns's Religion and Intellectual Milieu

Burns was subject, in the small villages and isolated farms that he lived in during his childhood and youth, to powerfully conflicting philosophical influences. The influence of the church was pervasive in rural Scotland. But the modern ideas of the Enlightenment were also very much present. It is significant that Burns's early readings included both theological writings and those of two important philosophers of the Enlightenment, John Locke and Adam Smith.

Burns's church was the Church of Scotland, also called Presbyterian. Its founder, John Calvin, argued that humans are so contaminated by Original Sin that only a few can be saved, and those only by the direct intervention and guidance of God. Reacting against late Renaissance emphasis on the freedom and dignity of man, he insisted that man is totally dependent on God and that God has foreordained all things, including the specific details of each individual's life. Hence the future of all people's souls, whether one goes to Heaven or to Hell after death, is predestined by God at the time of birth. The "Elect," those people who are predestined to go to Heaven, Calvin argued, will live virtuous lives because God has foreordained it and because they alone have God's assistance in living rightly. Good deeds are not enough for salvation. One must believe in Christ, in the Bible, and in the teachings of Calvin because they offer the only way to resist sin. Disbelief in any part of them is a sign that one will not have the help needed for salvation.

In the early eighteenth century, many Presbyterians, influenced by Enlightenment thinkers, began to question the doctrine of predestination. They were particularly influenced by the idea, called "universalism," which said that all people have certain essential similarities. It was only a small step for them to develop the belief that Christians were not inherently different from non-Christians. The Evangelicals, the "Auld Lichts," believed that certain people were born morally superior, that their election by God made them intrinsically different from all others. The Moderates, the "New Lichts," believed that more virtuous behavior was the result of better training.

The Enlightenment's argument for universalism was not the only influence that caused the Moderates to challenge the doctrine of predestination. But because of universalism, the challenge emerges, in the Moderate Presbyterian doctrine, with a more liberal tone than it generally had had in earlier forms of Christianity and with broader implications. The Moderates' belief in universalism had something in common with the popular late-eighteenth-century political belief in equality and the brotherhood of man.

The two factions stereotyped and condemned each other. The Evangelicals accused the Moderates of Deism, agnosticism, heresy, and immorality. The Moderates accused the Evangelicals of pride, pietism, and antinomianism—the doctrine that argued that a member of the Elect could sin as much as he pleased because he was predestined for salvation no matter what he did and because salvation depended on faith, not on virtuous acts.

In Burns's time the Moderates controlled the General Assembly, the ruling body of the national church, but the local churches were usually ruled by ministers and elders who were Evangelicals. The Kirk Session, the local ecclesiastical court that had direct influence on the daily life of the parishioners, was usually controlled by Evangelicals. This Kirk Session could and did pry into every aspect of the parishioners' lives and meted out punishment—fines, rebukes, public humiliation, temporary excommunication—for such offenses as working on the sabbath, not attending church regularly, expressing heterodox views, or fornication. For example, if a woman became pregnant out of wedlock both she and her lover were required to stand on a stool before the congregation, dressed in sackcloth, for three Sundays in a row and listen to the ministers' harangue.

Such meddling, self-righteous denial of personal and intellectual freedom obviously offended Burns, both personally and ideologically. Burns's father was a Moderate and Burns had been raised as one. His personal inclination would be to oppose the doctrine of predestination in any case and to oppose oppression in all forms.

Yet there were two sides to the issue, as Burns acknowledges in his poetry. The Moderates often brought an aloofness and a lack of passion to the pulpit. They had the reputation, often deserved, of cold, intellectual preaching, which was far from the hell-fire, intense preachings the rural parishioners were used to and which formed a large part of their lives. Calvinism viewed most pleasures as sinful, while the poverty of the villages made many pleasures out of the reach of peasants. But one pleasure was allowed and available, the pleasure of intense, blood-warming, and heart-warming religious services. The Moderates, with their rationalism, wanted to take that away and give little in its place except intellectual, abstract theology.

The Evangelical belief that only Presbyterians would go to Heaven is not an attractive one for most of us. But the Moderates' views had some of the taint of the excessive emphasis on "reason" that Burns, in other contexts, objected to. The Evangelicals upheld a religion that was warmer, more passionate, more immediately gratifying. They believed in a kind of passion that Burns, in other contexts, also believed in. This theological and personal conflict between opposing ideas and experiences, between, in simple terms, Burns's reason and passion, infuses and intensifies much of his poetry.

A second conflict in the ideas of the period was between the Christian doctrine of Original Sin and the Enlightenment doctrine of benevolism, the belief that human beings are essentially good. Almost all Presbyterians, Moderates and Evangelicals, believed that man is basically evil, that Original Sin has given him an intrinsic propensity

to vice that requires Christian guidance and regular vigilance to com-
bat. The Moderates usually accepted the doctrine of universalism. But
they united with the Evangelicals in their opposition to the belief in
intrinsic virtue and the denial of Original Sin.

Writers of the Enlightenment, in particular mid-century Scottish
writers such as David Hume and Adam Smith, argued that human
beings have desirable intrinsic qualities—they called them "passions"—such as generosity, kindness, and friendship. The degree of
personal religious commitment varied among the different writers, but
they all agreed that people could live reasonably virtuous lives without
constant effort and without God's constant help.

Many inferences were drawn from this idea of man's intrinsic virtue.
If man is essentially good, then his inner sense will tell him how to
live a virtuous life. Instead of praying for divine guidance or following
church teachings or social conventions, he need only consult his own
feelings. Since evil in the world could not be attributed to man's intrinsic propensity to vice, then society must be the culprit. Education,
the manners of civilized society, the arts, all became suspect. The less
contact one has with civilization, the better one is likely to be. The
best person was the simplest person—a child who has not yet been
corrupted by society, a beggar or gypsy who lives outside of conventional society and social norms, the noble savage, and, most frequently,
the peasant, the person who is close to the soil, close to nature.

The idea that man is essentially good (and its corollary, that feelings
are more reliable than reason or tradition) comes from numerous
sources—from England and from France, from seventeenth-century
Christians and from eighteenth-century Deists, from Shaftesbury, Bolingbroke, Hume, Smith, and Rousseau. It took numerous forms and
came in various degrees of intensity. Some argued that man was not
quite as bad as the doctrine of Original Sin would seem to make him.
Others argued that man was all good and only society was evil. But
the idea that man was not intrinsically evil powerfully influenced a
great many people in the late eighteenth century, and it powerfully
influenced Burns.

The idea came to Burns from many sources. It occurs frequently in
much of the eighteenth-century writing that we know Burns read and
admired, in the poetry of Pope, Shenstone, Thomson, Gray, and Allan
Ramsay, in the essays of Addison, Steele, and Henry Mackenzie, in the
novels of Sterne, Smollett, and Mackenzie, and in Adam Smith's *Theory
of Moral Sentiments*. And we can find it in a more austere form in the

writings of Locke, who was probably the major influence on the writers of the Enlightenment, and thus influenced Burns both directly and indirectly. The idea was everywhere.

Many of the characters in Burns's poetry personify this idea of benevolism. The rustic individualist, the peasant woman at her spinning wheel, the young woman who has been deserted by her lover, the poet who writes outside the mainstream, the beggars who create their own social and ethical structure, the poor farmer who has little other than his own struggles to provide him with guidance are examples of the new hero. He is outside the mainstream of society, uneducated, uncultivated, a natural human being.

Burns also expresses benevolism through the use of commonplace experiences and ordinary emotions. In his descriptions of sitting in church, working on the farm, drinking and singing with friends, spending an evening with a cotter's family, wondering about love, wandering in the woods, examining one's own desires and conflicts, he expresses what Carol McGuirk calls the "dogmatic defense of secular spontaneity."[4] The subject matter for his poetry comes out of the everyday experience of the essentially good person.

In August 1785, early in his writing career, Burns wrote a version of "Green Grow the Rashes," in his *Commonplace Book* including the famous chorus:

> Green grow the rashes—O
> Green grow the rashes—O
> The sweetest hours that e'er I spend,
> Are spent among the lasses—O.

He added the comment, "I do not see that the turn of mind, and pursuits of such a one as the above verses describe . . . but he may gain Heaven."[5] The statement is awkward and tentative. But he develops the implications of this idea throughout his life, in particular his doubts about the concept of Original Sin. Apparently, at the time that he was writing the poetry for his first volume, he was beginning to have doubts about certain Christian tenets and to think seriously about benevolism.

His prose comments speak clearly of his belief that humans are born intrinsically good and are corrupted by society. For example, he says, "We come into this world with a heart & disposition to do good for it, untill by dashing a large mixture of base alloy called Prudence alias

Selfishness, the too precious Metal of the Soul is brought down to the blackguard Sterling of ordinary currency" (R 261). But his poetry does not always reflect such a favorable view of human nature.

Burns's Presbyterian teachings never left him, and he saw too much of harsh reality to give full credence to the belief in intrinsic virtue. The heroes of his writing are not weak people who must struggle with their innate vices, but neither are they virtuous, kind, sweet people who do good by instinct. Beggars, for example, readily turn on one another when they get the chance. They are no better and no worse than anyone else. Society is sometimes portrayed as a cause of human evil, but it is not the only cause. The harm we do to one another more often appears in his poetry as the result of the way people are.

Part of Burns's strength as a poet comes from his ability to express these conflicts: between the universalism of the Moderate Presbyterians and the concrete intensity of the Evangelicals; between the benevolism of the Enlightenment and the grimmer view of a harsh reality that came from his experience. His ability to express these conflicting ideas simultaneously gives a particular dimension to the richness of his poetic statement.

Burns had the good fortune to inherit two literary traditions, the Scottish and the English, which spoke with different voices and in different styles. The Scottish Literary Revival gave him a particular style that he was able to combine with the English tradition to express the complex and contradictory vision of his confused age.

The Scottish Literary Revival

Burns's Scotland was a country that was struggling to maintain its identity and its cohesion, in danger of being submerged by the culture of its richer, more powerful neighbor to the south. The similarities and differences between Scotland and England of the late eighteenth century—and now—are not easy to define. England and most of Scotland spoke different dialects of the same language. They had one Parliament, one King, and closely related legal systems. Both countries were Protestant. But Scotland had a distinctive history that was as ancient as England's. It had been a financially and militarily self-sufficient country with a great intellectual and literary tradition, a distinctive culture, and a history of proud independence. It was in no way prepared to have its identity submerged into that of its larger southern neighbor.

Scotland had, over the previous two centuries, gradually become politically united with England. When Queen Elizabeth died, James VI of Scotland, of the House of Stuart, became heir to the throne of England as James I, so that in 1603 the crowns of both countries were united. The royal families became one permanently. Even before the Union of Crowns, Scotland had been converting to Calvinism under the leadership of John Knox. Knox adopted an English version of the Bible and encouraged stronger affiliation with Protestant England than with Catholic France. The new contact encouraged the use of standard English for religious services as well as for Bible reading.

And then, in 1707, the two countries united politically in the Act of Union. The Union meant that Scotland would dissolve its own Parliament and send members to the Parliament in London. Those who voted for the Union believed it would bring economic advantages. Whether it did is still debatable. But what is not debatable is that the act brought Scotland even further under the influence of England and further diminished its sense of individuality. Inevitably, more powerful, more populous England gained cultural as well as political ascendancy.

Further humiliations were in store. The British crown had continued to be held by the House of Stuart, so the Scots could at least console themselves with knowing that a family of Scottish descent and with a Scottish name ruled the two kingdoms. But in 1714 Queen Anne died without heir, and the crown passed to her German cousins, the Hanovers. George I and George II were no more English than they were Scottish, but the English did not need such symbols to give them a sense of identity. The Scots, in a desperate attempt to regain this symbolic superiority to England, took actions that only made matters worse.

The descendants of James II, who had been deposed by the British in 1688, had continued to claim their right to the British throne. Prince Charles Stuart, the pretender to the British throne, had supporters in both England and Scotland, called "Jacobites." In 1745 he attempted to invade England from Scotland, supported by Highland troops. His supporters were defeated at the Battle of Culloden; Prince Charles ran back to Italy; and the Scottish supporters were left to pay for their rebellion. The English outlawed the tartans and the bagpipes and placed some economic sanctions on the Highland industries. These bans were lifted during Burns's lifetime and were difficult to enforce at any time. But they served, along with the demise of the House of

Stuart and the defeat at Culloden, to remind Scotland of its position of military weakness and subservience to England.

And in 1760, George III, English born and bred, became king of England and Scotland. Scotland still had its distinctive dialect, its local customs, its literary tradition, and its separate church. But all these institutions were threatened in some way. The danger was that the smaller, poorer country would become overwhelmed. Its language would become only a local dialect; its intellectual, literary, and artistic traditions would be absorbed by the English traditions; its beautiful, historic capital, Edinburgh, would become another provincial town; and the entire country would become a mere appendage to its neighbor.

The situation was further complicated by the division within Scotland itself, between Lowlands and Highlands, which spoke different languages. The language of the Lowlands of Scotland (i.e., southern and northeastern Scotland), the language Burns spoke, descended from the language spoken by the same Teutonic tribes that had populated England in the early Middle Ages. Lowlands Scottish, called "Lallan," was in the Middle Ages, in Burns's time, and is now, a dialect of English. It has regional differences in vocabulary, grammar, and pronunciation from the language spoken in England, but it is still the same language. In the Highlands—the mountainous area of northwestern Scotland—and in the western islands of Scotland, the language spoken was Scottish Gaelic, the language spoken by the Celts who had originally inhabited all of what is now Scotland. It is only distantly related to the language spoken in the Lowlands.

The division between Highlands and Lowlands was more than linguistic. The Highlanders were a prefeudal people, primarily sheep and cattle herders, divided into warring clans. Many of the symbols we associate with Scotland, the tartans, kilts, bagpipes, and clan organization, are of Highland origin. The Lowlanders tended to be agricultural or urban, peace-loving, industrious, and settled. The Highlanders tended to go their own way, maintaining a glorious island of medievalism. The Lowlanders were more influenced by continental European ideas, especially those of France—in the sixteenth and seventeenth centuries by the French Renaissance, in the eighteenth century by the Enlightenment. They maintained and developed intellectual and literary affiliations with England. The division created problems. But Highlands and Lowlands were still one country.

Burns was a fervent Scottish patriot. He reports that in his early years, possibly the early teens, he read the history of William Wallace, which "poured a Scotish prejudice in my veins which will boil along there till the flood-gates of life shut in eternal rest" (R 125). His commitment to Scottish patriotism runs throughout his writings, and he repeatedly expresses resentment of English encroachment on Scottish ways and his commitment to Scottish literature.

Scottish writers, especially Robert Fergusson, exerted a profound influence on his writings. He reports that when he was twenty-three, "meeting with Fergusson's Scotch poems, I strung anew my wildly-sounding, rustic lyre with emulating vigour" (R 125). Burns's statement serves as a focus to express his relationship to the entire Scottish Revival of the eighteenth century.

In the fifteenth and early sixteenth centuries, Scottish literature, with such writers as William Dunbar, Robert Henryson, Gavin Douglas, and David Lyndsay, formed one of the great literary traditions of Europe. But the tradition declined and all but disappeared. In the early eighteenth century, however, the Scottish Literary Revival started, growing out of the Scotsmen's need to reassert their country's individuality, out of their somewhat blurred sense of their country's great literary past, and out of a general European interest in nationalism and folk traditions. This revival provided Burns with several sources of Scottish poetry—newly published collections of older poetry, collections of songs, and original poetry published throughout the century—which he read, admired, and used for models for the language, forms, imagery, and subject matter of his own writing.

The revival was Scottish in style and intent yet was influenced by certain literary and political trends that were British or European in origin. What is particular to Scotland, however, is that these trends took literary root in that country and flourished in a way that did not occur elsewhere.

One major European trend was nationalism. The special characteristics that made each country unique were a growing subject of interest throughout Europe. In Scotland, however, this trend served the additional purpose of providing a way for the people to express their country's separation from England and to resist the growing tendency to submerge Scotland into English culture. The revival in literature provided one especially important way for Scotland to express its individuality and its nationalist pride.

An aspect of the revival was the publication, throughout the eighteenth century, of several collections of Scottish poetry and songs:

James Watson's *Choice Collection of Comic and Serious Scots Poems*, published in 1706, 1709, and 1711; Allan Ramsay's *Tea-Table Miscellany*, published 1724–27, and *Evergreen*, published in 1724; and David Herd's *Ancient and Modern Scottish Songs, Heroic Ballads etc.*, published in 1769 and revised in 1776. Watson's *Choice Collection*, started just a year before the Union with England, expressed a new awareness of a tradition that could assert Scottish literary independence. Watson announced in his preface that it was "The first of its Nature which has been publish'd in our own Native *Scots* Dialect." Herd, writing in the preface to his edition of 1776, said, "The Scots yield to none of their neighbors in their passionate attachment to their native music; in which, to say the truth, they seem to be justified by the unbiased suffrage of foreigners of the best taste." Other attempts were made, in other countries, to assert the sense of national character through a literary tradition. But none was more successful in the eighteenth century than the revival in Scotland.

The revival of Scottish literature served the further nationalistic purpose of lending honor to the language of Scotland. Most of the intellectual and social elite of Scotland looked on their native language as provincial and, in spite of their genuine patriotism, strove to rid their speech of localisms in grammar, vocabulary, and pronunciation in order to speak the English spoken by educated Englishmen. The poets of the revival, on the other hand, chose to write in a form of Scottish because it was the language they believed had been used by older Scottish poets and was the language of their own country.

Actually, the language they wrote in was neither. The language of the medieval Scottish poets was courtly and elegant; the language of the revival purported to be colloquial. But the eighteenth-century writers paid little attention to the medieval poets and misread them when they did.[6] Ramsay's *Evergreen*, which published the older poetry, received far less attention than his more modern collection, *Tea-Table Miscellany*.[7] The poets seemed less interested in the style and language of the Scottish tradition than in the patriotism it expressed symbolically. Their written language was the language Burns often used for his best poetry.

The language they wrote in was not that of the common man nor, in fact, the language that Burns or anyone else actually spoke. It was a literary language, combining elements of older Scottish diction, contemporary colloquial Scottish of various dialects, spoken sophisticated

Scottish, spoken English, and literary English.[8] Writers cheerfully included forms that were grammatical English but ungrammatical Scottish, forms that did not exist in Scottish but looked like Scottish equivalents of English (e.g., "wham" for whom"), or interchanged Scottish and English words when the exchange helped the rhyme or the meter. The language was, as John Butt says, "a common denominator of Scottish dialects [laced] with English poetic diction. . . . the modern equivalent of Doric appropriately used for a just representation of rural manners."[9] The Scottish of the revival was not a re-creation of a native tradition, but a symbolic act to suggest a new nationalism. And the Scottish diction also provided the poets with an idiom to express the new, popular interest in the common man.

This interest in the life of the ordinary person, especially the peasant, grew partly out of the literary doctrine that what was natural and simple was best, partly out of the fledgling social sciences—a kind of protoanthropology, and partly out of the democratic political trends occurring in Europe and America. The folk song provided an obvious source of literature that dealt with the life of the common person. Collecting and editing songs became an interest of both English and Scottish editors, such as Ramsay and Watson. Burns was to follow this trend and become one of the greatest song collectors and editors in British history. But the interest in peasant life had another, rather intriguing origin.

Matthew MacDiarmid writes, "Modern Scots poetry begins in the seventeenth century as a literary joke, an entertainment of the same order as macaronic or Hudibrastic verse. . . . a comic play with undignified language, a species of burlesque."[10] Allan Ramsay, the editor of *Tea-Table Miscellany*, was also a poet. He continued this comic tradition, writing about rustic life as if it were a subject of amused condescension, the sort of behavior a gentleman might joke about while accepting it as appropriate for the lower orders. This awkward and rather unappealing style might have continued if it had not been altered by another influence, this time from England.

Alexander Pope and John Gay had been involved in a literary dispute with Joseph Addison, Ambrose Phillips, and others, over the nature of the pastoral. Pope and Gay believed that the pastoral should portray an ideal world; Addison and Phillips believed that it should portray a realistic one. In defense of their position, Pope wrote a satirical essay for *Guardian* 40, ironically praising the virtues of pastorals about low

rustic life. Gay wrote a satirical pastoral, *The Shepherds' Week*, that ironically followed the rules of Pope. But Gay's poem, like his other works,
The Beggars' Opera and *Trivia*, was too good humored, too accepting to
come off completely as satire.

Ramsay knew the works of Gay and Pope. A few years after publication of *The Shepherds's Week* he published *Patie and Roger* and *The
Gentle Shepherd*, which indicate the influence of Gay's work and demonstrate that Ramsay, like most of Gay's readers, took *The Shepherds's
Week* seriously and possibly took Pope's *Guardian* 40 seriously.[11] In
these pastorals Ramsay began to treat peasant life with less condescension than he had in his earlier pastorals and to portray it sympatheti-
cally, even with loving detail. Though Ramsay was not an especially
good poet or good editor, through his enthusiasm, energy, and oppor-
tunism, he did much to create the Scottish Revival. His editions of
Scottish poetry and his original writings, which began truly to reflect
Scottish rustic life, became enormously popular in Scotland among all
classes. As David Daiches says, "He restored Scots literature to its natural place in the daily life of the people by associating it with the
normal activities of the citizen."[12]

The most interesting aspect of these events is not the complicated
influences of eighteenth-century literary history, but the fact that these
ideas took root in Scotland and not in England. The trend in England,
at this time, was toward the universality of human nature. In English
poetry the writer tried to express experience in terms that avoided excessive particularity. Samuel Johnson had Imlac say, in *Rasselas*: "The
business of a poet . . . is to examine, not the individual, but the species; to remark general properties and large appearances; he does not
number the streaks of the tulip. . . . He must divest himself of the
prejudices of his age or country. . . . He must write as the interpreter
of nature . . . as a being superior to time and place" (chapter 10).

Thomas Gray describes the dead peasant's surviving family in his
"Elegy Written in a Country Churchyard," reflecting his benevolist
(and sentimental) ideas and his style of generality:

> For them no more the blazing hearth shall burn,
> Or busy housewife ply her evening care.
> No children run to lisp their sire's return,
> Or climb his knee the envied kiss to share.
>
> (ll. 21–24)

From mid-century onward, English poetry had little of the particularity, the concrete detail of ordinary life, especially peasant life, as one finds everywhere in Scottish poetry. For example, from Ramsay:

For here yestreen I brew'd a bow of maut;	*last evening; bowl; malt*
Yestreen I slew twa wethers prime and fat;	*two gelded pigs*
A furlet of good cakes my Elspa beuk,	*bundle; baked*
And a large ham hings reesting in the nook.	
("The Gentle Shepherd" 2.1)	

Ramsay's poetry, in general, leaves something to be desired. But he had created a style that restored seriousness to Scottish poetry while maintaining its popularity, its broad appeal, and its range of familiar subject matter. Other poets were to follow Ramsay and improve upon him, most notably, Robert Fergusson.

Just why this style took root in the Scottish tradition is debatable. Many have speculated on the Scottish "national character,"[13] or on the "oral literary culture which had deep roots in the past,"[14] or on a largely imaginary continuous Scottish tradition.[15] Such speculations have their use. But a more demonstrable relationship can be seen in the similarity between the style of the revival and the style of the Scottish folk song.

The Scottish folk song, in its earlier and eighteenth-century forms, has the remarkable concreteness, the down-to-earth, no-nonsense, unsentimental approach to ordinary life that is to characterize the poetry of Scotland. For example:

My daddie is a cankert carle,	*peevish old man*
He'll no twine wi' his gear	*part*
My minnie, she's a scaudin' wife,	*mother; scolding*
Hauds a' the house asteer.	*holds; turmoil*
("Low doun in the broom," Anon.)	

In the eighteenth century the folk song enjoyed greater popularity in Scotland than in England. The reason may be as MacDiarmid speculates, that Scottish folk songs about rustic life prospered because the "country-folk and working-class . . . had the chance to find their own voice."[16] In England the continuous literary tradition prevented such a development. As a result, eighteenth-century Scottish poets of the

revival, Allan Ramsay, William Hamilton of Gilbertfield, Alexander
Ross, William Hamilton of Bangour, John Skinner, Robert Fergusson,
Robert Burns, and others, found, in the rich source of local folk songs,
a genuine, current Scottish style on which to model the subject matter,
imagery, and often the forms of their own poetry. They did not generally use the medieval Scottish tradition as a source, but they did
know about the folk song. Between the ideas of Gay's *Shepherd's Week*
and the methods of the Scottish folk song, they found a distinctive
style to express their love of Scotland.

Robert Fergusson wrote the best poetry in this tradition before
Burns and exerted the single most important Scottish influence on
him. Fergusson lived mostly in Edinburgh, where he led an impoverished, bohemian life. Many people in Scotland recognized him as an
important poet, but no one gave him financial help. He had to continue at a dreary clerical job and died in 1774, profoundly depressed
and in poverty. Burns felt considerable identification with this wild,
tormented, highly talented poet who was recognized but inadequately
appreciated, and he used much of Fergusson's poetry as a model for his
own style.

Although Fergusson is a poet of city life, his feeling for the commonplace far transcends the difference between country and city. As
Alan MacLaine says, "With his keen eye for concrete detail and with
his wonderfully expressive command of the vernacular, he is able to
reveal in a few brief lines the whole reality of the scene and to suggest
with striking clarity and precision its characteristic atmosphere and
feeling."[17]

Burns finds in Fergusson's work, "The same home-felt themes of
poverty and unrewarding work, and unrecognized merit, heightening
the same pleasures of good-fellowship, drink, and song, and the op-
portunities of 'fine remarkin' on every feature of the local scene."[18]
From Fergusson Burns learned to express pride of place, applying Fergusson's love of the streets and taverns of Edinburgh to the farms and
inns of Ayrshire. And he learned to express his genuine Scottish patriotism, without Ramsay's condescension or apology, from Fergusson's
racy directness.

Burns frequently links Fergusson with Ramsay in acknowledging his
debt, as in the preface to his first edition of poetry, the Kilmarnock,
where he says, "Those two justly admired Scotch Poets he has often
had in his eye in the following pieces; but rather with a view to kindle
at their flame, than for servile imitation." He mentions Ramsay, but

he feels the greater debt to Fergusson, to whom he refers, in comparison with Ramsay, as the "still more excellent Ferguson" (*First Commonplace Book*, 36).

Yet Fergusson for all his richness of detail, rarely goes beyond description. His effective re-creation of a moment occurs in any number of his poems. For example:

> You crack weel o' your lasses there,   *boast*
> Their glancin een and bisket bare;   *eyes; breast*
> But thof this town be *smeekit* sair,   *though; smoky, sore*
>   I'll wad a *farden*,   *wage; farthing*
> Than ours they're nane mair fat and fair,   *none; more*
>   Cravin your pardon.
> ("Answer *to Mr* J. S.'s Epistle," ll.43–48)

Fergusson re-creates the moment, the scene, and the feeling, but no more than that. Neither in these nor in his other poems does he get beyond the present instant. His ability to preserve the concrete experience offers a relief from the abstractions of much of contemporary English poetry. But Burns, as we shall see, captures the moment equally well and also goes on to give it a rich symbolism.

Burns was in a position to profit by inheriting the two traditions—the abstract, symbolic English tradition, and the concrete, earthy Scottish tradition of the Revival and the folk song. The combination of the two would have been invigorating under any circumstances. But coming at this moment, when so many conflicting ideas—his personal conflicts and the European philosophical conflicts—needed expression, the combination offered an extraordinary opportunity. The opportunity was offered to other Scottish poets of the period, but it took a poet of Burns's genius to exploit it with such historic success.

Chapter Two

The Satiric and Moral Poetry

The Beginnings of His Career

Burns "first committed the sin of Rhyme" (R 125) in 1774, at the age of fifteen, when he wrote a song for a "bonie, sweet, sonsie lass." But during the next several years he wrote only a handful of works—a few good songs and some rather bad poems, somber expressions of his recurring depression, written in a style that was derived from contemporary English sentimental poetry. At some point, after 1782, his production began to increase. Starting in early 1785, when he was twenty-six, it became prodigious.

In July 1786, he published his first book, entitled *Poems Chiefly in the Scottish Dialect,* printed in the nearby town of Kilmarnock. It has since been known as "The Kilmarnock Edition." He had written most of the poems included in it over the previous eighteen months.

This unusual acceleration in productivity probably resulted from changes in the circumstances of his life. In 1777, when Burns was eighteen, the financially disastrous lease at Mt. Oliphant ended, and the family moved to a farm at Lochlie, where they lived in less poverty. He had a little more leisure time, and his reading increased. He read most of Pope, some Shakespeare, Locke's *Essay concerning Human Understanding,* and the works of Allan Ramsay. By 1782 he had read several works that he mentions as influential on himself—some novels of Sterne and Mackenzie and the poetry of Thomson, Shenstone, and Fergusson. He also read "a collection of letters by the Wits of Queen Ann's reign," Richardson's *Pamela,* and some novels of Smollett. In 1783 he quoted Adam Smith's *Theory of Moral Sentiments,* which he probably had read.

In 1780, Burns, his brother Gilbert, and five other young men formed a debating society, called the Tarbolton Bachelors' Club. They discussed such topics as "Whether do we derive more happiness from Love or Friendship" and "Whether is the savage man or the peasant of a civilized country in the most happy situation." The topics seem naive, but they covered subjects that were taken seriously by educated and sophisticated people throughout contemporary Europe and America. In 1781 he spent several months in a nearby town, Irvine, in a financially unsuccessful attempt at being a business man. He met a sailor there, Richard Brown, who Burns says, had "a knowledge of the world . . . vastly superior to mine" (R 125). Brown seems to have helped Burns to rid himself of some of his Calvinist restraints, especially in regard to women. Brown also appreciated Burns's poems. Burns had been writing them casually, as an amusement. Brown urged him to publish them. Then, in 1784, Burns's father died, and the family moved to another farm, at Mossgiel. It is around this time that he began writing his most important poetry. Scarcely more than a year later he had written all of the important poems of the Kilmarnock Edition.

These events are probably all significant. A number of experiences helped to liberate Burns from the parochialism and repressiveness of the Scottish village: the topics discussed by the debating society, his friendship with Brown, and, possibly, the death of his father. The readings in contemporary British literature, the works of Pope, Thomson, Shenstone, Sterne, Mackenzie, and Adam Smith influenced the ideas of the Kilmarnock volume, especially the ideas of benevolism and universalism. The reading of Pope, Thomson, and the writers of the Scottish Revival, Fergusson in particular, gave him important models for much of his best style.

Burns made the decision to publish his poems partly for financial reasons. He planned to emigrate to Jamaica, seeing that change as the only way to break away from the poverty of Scottish farming and the repressiveness of Scottish village life. He hoped that the royalties would pay for his passage. In addition, he had fathered a child by Betty Paton, and he wanted to leave her provided for. The book, however, turned out to be far more successful than he had expected, and the planned emigration never took place.

Most of the poems of the Kilmarnock Edition tend to be satiric and moral. They have an ethical position to argue from and advocate—the praise of freedom and spontaneity or the denunciation of repression, hypocrisy, and social and economic inequality. These poems are among his greatest works, but they represent a departure from the style of his writing generally. Before 1785, his few good works had been songs. After the publication of the Kilmarnock Edition all his best works, with the important exception of "Tam o'Shanter," were songs. For some reason, during the period from late 1784 to early 1786, Burns wrote in a different style from the rest of his career.

Burns's anger certainly plays some role in motivating this style. This anger, as we noted in the previous chapter, was directed at the social and economic system that had subjected him and his family to the hardship at Mt. Oliphant and at the repressions of the local Presbyterian Church. His anger at economic inequality had reason to continue after he left Mt. Oliphant because his financial situation at Lochlie and Mossgiel, while better than before, was still precarious. His expectation when he was writing these poems was that he would be a poor, struggling farmer all of his life.

The ideas of contemporary British writing, of the Enlightenment, and of the Scottish Revival offered him alternatives, ways to deal with the oppressions and stresses he suffered. Some leisure, intellectual stimulation, personal liberation, and grief probably all combined to motivate this outburst of satiric and moral poetry. The conflict of the English and Scottish traditions provides it with its particular shape. His genius, however, explains the innovativeness and originality of the poems of the Kilmarnock Edition.

The subject matter of the poetry includes the theme of conflict between poetry written "clean aff loof" (off-hand)—and poetry "writ by rule"; between wealth and poverty; between a free, unconventional style of life and prudence; between the rights of the individual and the repressions of the class system; between a religion "of the heart" and a religion of law; between sexual freedom and sexual repression. The ideas are not original. Everyone was writing in praise of freedom. Burns's contribution is in his translation of popular ideas into a vivid poetic style and in his expression of them as alternatives to hardship and repression. His contribution is also in his expansion of existing forms to make them more appropriate vehicles of these current ideas.

The Verse Epistles

Burns's development of the verse epistles written in 1784–85 and published in the Kilmarnock Edition demonstrates one way in which he grappled with these new, popular ideas and expressed them poetically. He followed the form of the Scottish verse epistle such as had been practiced by Allan Ramsay, William Hamilton of Gilbertfield, and Robert Fergusson. It usually starts with a eulogy, expresses admiration for the recipient, especially his poetry, and ends with a hope that the writer and recipient will meet and spend a convivial evening together. Like most poetry of the Scottish Revival, it is written in a mixture of Scottish and English, in a conversational, informal diction. It deals with familiar subjects and is personal and emotional: "When I receiv'd thy kind epistle/It made me dance, and sing, and whistle" ("Epistle II," Hamilton of Gilbertfield to Allan Ramsay). It includes familiar domestic Scottish details, "Eithly [easily] wou'd I be in your debt / A pint o' paritch [porridge]" (Fergusson, *Answer to Mr. J.S.'s Epistle*). And it is usually written in the "Standard Habbie" verse form, which is to become the most usual and successful of Burns's stanzas.

In one of his earlier epistles, "Epistle to Davie, a Brother Poet" (K 51),[1] written in late 1784 and early 1785, Burns includes many of his standard themes. (The poem is not written in the Standard Habbie verse form of his other verse epistles but in the meter of "The Cherry and the Slae," a medieval Scottish poem known to Burns.) Both poets, Burns and the recipient, David Sillar, are poor, which makes Burns "grudge a wee the *Great-folk's* gift" (l. 9). But their life has its compensations—the ability to enjoy a particular moment, the enjoyment of nature, the pleasures of writing poetry, and the pleasures of love.

He expresses the difficulties of being poor, "To lye in kilns and barns at e'en, / When banes are craz'd, and bluid is thin, / Is, doubtless, great distress" (ll. 29–31). Burns does not follow the contemporary, shallow theme that poverty is ennobling. But when he offers an alternative, the poem becomes abstract, "Yet then *content* could make us blest; / Ev'n then, sometimes we'd snatch a taste / Of truest happiness." The sense of a moment of true happiness that can come when least expected is an experience that we have all had. But Burns never conveys what this "truest happiness" is for him. He relies on the readers' experience.

In several of the following stanzas the poetry becomes derivative of various eighteenth-century poems, like Thomson's *Castle of Indolence,* in, "Yet *Nature's* charms, the hills and woods, / The sweeping vales, and foaming floods, / Are free alike to all" (ll. 46–48). Well, yes. But we all know that. What does Burns get from the "sweeping vales" and "foaming floods"? He tells us nothing that conveys the personal joy he claims to have. Later, the poem gets worse, "All hail! ye tender feelings dear! / The smile of love, the friendly tear" (ll. 127–28). But in the last stanza the poem comes marvelously to life. He has mentioned Jean, his love, and then:

> O, how that *name* inspires my style!
> The words come skelpin, rank and file,   *rushing, skipping*

Amaist before I ken!   *almost; know*
The ready measure rins as fine,   *runs*
As *Phoebus* and the famous *Nine*
    Were glowran owre my pen.   *staring intently; over*
My spavet *Pegasus* will limp,   *spavined*
    Till ance he's fairly het;   *once; hot, excited*
And then he'll hilch, and stilt, and jimp,   *lurch; prance; jump*
    And rin an unco fit;   *run; wondrous*
But least then, the beast then,   *lest*
    Should rue this hasty ride,
I'll light now, and dight now,   *wipe down*
    His sweaty, wizen'd hide.

In this stanza Burns strikes his best style. He has been talking about the alternatives to the hardships of poverty and an unfair social system: freedom, nature, poetry writing, friendship, and love. When he mentions the last one, his love for Jean, he translates his emotional response into the physical description of the words jumping and skipping. Then he uses the same image of irregular physical movement to express his creative impulse, describing the movements of his imaginary Pegasus who, in a frenzy of amorous and creative excitement, lurches, prances, jumps, and gets into "an unco fit." The movements of the words and of Pegasus convey the sensations that just about everyone has in like circumstances. Burns expresses his feelings of love and creative inspiration by relating them to recognizable, amusing physical counterparts.

Burns ironically uses classical mythology. By the eighteenth century, classical mythology had been worked to death. Some poets, such as Gray and Collins, attempted to alter and refresh the old myths. Others, such as Pope, used the myths for satiric and comic effects. Burns follows Pope but adds the element of familiar irreverence. His use of Apollo and the Muses ("*Phoebus* and the famous *Nine*") and Pegasus allows him to make a fond connection to the ancient western tradition. His bantering, amiable tone allows him to present his poetry as the product of a poet who writes out of his instant emotions and who does not take himself or the tradition very seriously. He can joke about himself, joke about the classical poetic tradition, joke about his own feelings, and still convey what those feelings are.

The techniques of describing the physical counterpart of his emotions, of joking about himself, and of using classical mythology ironically all convey the alternatives to lying in a cold barn with crazed bones: the pleasures of love and creativity conveyed with self-humor and spontaneity.

The style of the epistles rapidly improved. "To the Same" (K 58), often called "Second Epistle to J. Lapraik," written in April 1785, only a few months after "Epistle to Davie," shows how far Burns has developed the form in such a short time. In this poem Burns uses the techniques of the final stanza of "Epistle to Davie" through most of the poem, making a far more consistent integration of ideas and style.

The first epistle to Lapraik, called "Epistle to J. L*****k, An Old Scotch Bard," was written after Burns heard some of Lapraik's poetry. It develops the themes of the simple life, spontaneous poetry, love, and friendship as the alternatives to the complex life of civilization with its rules for writing, its demand for classical learning, and its repressive sexual morality. "To the same" was written in response to Lapraik's answer. It follows the same themes but develops them.

The verse form that Burns uses for this epistle and for many of his most successful poems is the Standard Habbie, a form he learned from Ramsay and Fergusson.[2] It is a six line stanza, with lines one, two, three, and five in rhyming iambic tetrameter, lines four and six in rhyming iambic dimeter. For example,

> Sae I gat paper in a blink,   *so; got*
> An' down gaed *stumpie* in the ink;   *went; stump of my pen*
> Quoth I, 'Before I sleep a wink,
>   'I vow I'll close it;
> 'An' if ye winna mak it clink,   *will not; rhyme*
>   'By Jove I'll prose it!'
>   (ll. 31–36)

The stanza allows Burns, as it had allowed his Scottish predecessors, to break from the heroic couplet that had dominated British poetry for more than a half century. Ramsay and Fergusson, however, did little to exploit the potential of the verse form beyond using it to give conversational rhythm. Burns uses the long lines to give a certain order and the short lines to create a slight unevenness, so that the stanza conveys, on one hand, a conversational rhythm, an easy, relaxed tone that is consistent with the theme of an unpremeditated poetry, and, on the other hand, a counterpoint of recurring order. The short line conveys a spontaneous afterthought, a nice turn of phrase, or an emotional aside, as, "By Jove I'll prose it!" or "But I shall scribble down some blether [nonsense] / Just clean aff-loof [off-hand]." The long lines, with their extended meter, greater substance, and more frequently repeated rhymes, provide a sense of order that balances the spontaneity.

Stanzas two to six are written as an argument with his muse. The passage starts:

Forjeskit sair, with weary legs,	*worn-out; sore*
Rattlin the corn out-owre the rigs,	*sowing wheat; ridges*
Or dealing thro' amang the naigs	*distributing; horses*
Their ten-hours bite,	
My awkwart Muse sair pleads and begs,	*cantankerous*
I would na write.	

His own physical weariness becomes the condition of his cantankerous, resisting muse. This witty analogue of a reluctant muse and a tired, momentarily uncreative poet expresses, in sensuous detail, Burns's experience in trying to write this epistle. But he overcomes his weariness by threatening his muse: " 'An' if ye winna mak it clink, / 'By Jove I'll prose it!' " (ll. 34–35). The result is that:

Sae I've begun to scrawl, but whether	*so*
In rhyme, or prose, or baith thegither,	*both together*
Or some hotch-potch that's rightly neither,	
Let time mak proof;	
But I shall scribble down some blether	*nonsense*
Just clean aff-loof.	*offhand*

The resolution of his inner struggle with his creative powers is to write "aff-loof," in an informal style, "In rhyme, or prose, or baith thegither." The dialogue with his muse, his irreverant description of her as a "tapetless, ramfeezl'd hizzie [heedless, worn-out hussy]," the familiar images as, "An down gaed *stumpie* [went the stump of my pen] in the ink," the chatty short lines, all help to give the sense of a poetry that comes right out of his thoughts, without rules, almost impulsive.

The idea of unpremeditated poetry was a common critical idea in Burns's time.[3] Burns, however, expands the idea of a natural, unerudite poetry into an expression of an entire way of life. He brings together his physical tiredness, the hard farm work, his resisting creative powers, his emotional need to express himself when his bodily and mental powers are inclined against it, his conflict between laziness and the need to work, his desire to reach out in friendship to a fellow poet, his attractive self-deprecation ("some hotch-potch" and "blether"), and the formal difficulty of creating rhymes rather than prose. He relates all these feelings to the process of writing poetry in a diction that sounds consistent for a rustic Scottish farmer, expressed freely and seemingly without premeditation. Spontaneous poetry is an example of the un-constrained and natural emotions that can be the alternative to the repressions of poverty and conventions.

Burns uses Scottish vocabulary and grammatical (or pseudogram-matical) forms to strengthen this particular voice. Some of the forms are just spellings of words the way an uneducated Scotsman might have pronounced them. Other cases illustrate the kind of raciness that sug-gests a farmer talking (e.g., "blether" or "aff-loof"). The effect is un-mistakable. We get the sense of chattiness, spontaneity, and of a rustic speaker.

He expands this metaphor further into the idea of creativity and friendship as a way of dealing with life's unfairness:

> My worthy friend, ne'er grudge an' carp,
> Tho' Fortune use you hard an' sharp;
> Come, kittle up your *moorlan harp*   *rouse; moorland*
>   Wi' gleesom touch!
> Ne'er mind how Fortune *waft* an' *warp;*
>   She's but a b-tch.
>
>   (ll. 43–48)

Burns denounces the undesirable repressive part of the world—the middle class "*city-gent,* / . . . purse-proud, big wi' cent per cent, / An' muckle wame [fat stomach]"(ll. 61—64) and the upper class, "paughty [insolent], feudal *Thane,* / Wi' ruffl'd sark [shirt] an' glancin cane" (ll. 67–68) and then states his alternative, asking that God " 'turn me, if *Thou*' please, *adrift,* / 'Thro' Scotland wide' " (ll. 75–76). He does not offer a political solution or advocate change of the economic or class system. Rather, his solution is to go outside the system by going "adrift / 'Thro' Scotland wide."

In the previous chapter we noted that Burns accepted intellectually the benevolist doctrine that people are basically good, but he still showed some uncertainty about it. His reservations come out clearly in his doubts about political solutions to human ills. He expressed support of the American Revolution and, in the early years, of the French Revolution. He wrote some political poems (e.g., "On the Death of the late Lord President Dundas," "Scots Wha Hae," and "For a' 'that and a' that") and often discussed political issues in his prose. But in general he avoids politics in his poetry. He never actually contradicts the common Enlightenment argument that people will behave well if present social and political institutions will stop corrupting them. But he often qualifies it. His solution to existing problems is not so much to change the political or social scheme as it is to escape from it.[4]

From this position stems his belief in salvation through individual, sexual, and creative freedom. He argues, consistently, that we all have certain strengths within us which we can experience through friendship, love, creativity, through just talking a walk in the woods. We have the power because we are decent and not corrupted by Original Sin. But the social and political system is not likely to improve much. So the solution is for each person to go, on his own, outside the system.

Only two stanzas later, however, Burns expresses agreement with the popular belief in a benevolent world and the adulation of the new hero, echoing Pope's *Essay on Man* (4. 341–60): " 'The social, friendly, honest man, / 'Whate'er he be, / ' 'Tis *he* fulfils *great Nature's plan*" (ll. 87–89). The passage does not seem very believable, partly because of the hollow ring of the borrowed diction, and partly because he contradicts the idea in the next stanza:

> O *Mandate,* glorious and divine!
> The followers o' the ragged Nine,
> Poor, thoughtless devils! yet may shine
>   In glorious light,
> While sordid sons o' Mammon's line
>   Are dark as night!
>   (ll. 91–96)

His reference to the muses as the "ragged Nine" and all poets as "poor, thoughtless devils" puts him and the entire Western poetic tradition among the outsiders, indifferent to *"great Nature's plan."* The image of their "light" is developed in the following stanza, continuing the contrast to "night":

> Tho' here they scrape, an' squeeze, an' growl,
> Their worthless nievefu' of a *soul,*   *fistful*

> May in some *future carcase* howl,
>   The forest's fright;
> Or in some day-detesting *owl*
>   May shun the light.
>
> (ll. 97–102)

The "squeeze" of the first line of the stanza applies to the souls of the "sordid sons o' Mammon's line" squeezed into a clenched fist, then into animals of the night, a howling carcase or a "day-detesting owl." The contrast is between a squeezed, repressed, light-shunning way of life and a way of life that is like writing "aff-loof," like wandering "adrift / 'Thro' Scotland wide," and like shining in "glorious light."

The final stanza follows the amusing metempsychosis of the previous one with a mock apotheosis of Burns and Lapraik:

> Then may L*****k and B**** arise,
> To reach their native, kindred skies,
> And *sing* their pleasures, hopes an' joys,
>   In some mild sphere,
> Still closer knit in friendship's ties
>   Each passing year!
>
> (ll. 103–9)

The stanza contrasts the "arise" of Burns and Lapraik with the repressive images of the "cits" and "lairds" in the previous stanza. Burns modestly limits himself and his friend to their "native, kindred skies . . . In some mild sphere" where, presumably, they "yet may shine."

Burns may be serious about "*great Nature's plan*" when he says it. But the structure of the epistle indicates that his heart is elsewhere. The poem ends with Burns and Lapraik, "followers o' the ragged nine," indifferent to large philosophical schemes, singing in a small, Scottish heaven. The emphasis on the resources of each person, the ones he can use to reach his personal freedom, has reached a considerably more consistent treatment in ideas and style in this poem than in "Epistle to Davie," written only three months earlier.

The epistle "To J.S****" (K 79), written in the winter of 1785–86, is perhaps his best. He has developed the technique as far as he is going to. The epistle appears to be aimless and unstructured, merely an informal, rambling note to a friend. But the poem is held together by its consistent theme and images. The theme, as in his other epistles, is the desirability of all kinds of freedom—personal, artistic, social, economic—as an alternative to the world's inevitable hardships of poverty, old age, the class system, and economic oppression. The images are those of unstructured movement—"vacant, careless roamin'," "We frisk away," "we wander there, we wander here," "nae rules nor roads observin'," "To right or left, eternal swervin"—opposed to the crabbed, premeditated movements of the "douse folk, that live by rule" and "ken the road," who "Fortune chase" with "steady aim," who "urge the race," "seize the prey," "never stray," who are "tideless-blooded," and whose "hearts are just a standing pool."

The first stanza opens with the compliment to the recipient that is conventional for the opening of a Scottish epistle:

Dear S****, the sleest, pawkie thief,	*slyest, crafty*
That e'er attempted stealth or rief,	*plunder*
Ye surely hae some warlock-breef	*warlock's charm*
Owre human hearts;	*over*
For ne'er a bosom yet was prief	*proof*
Against your arts.	

The second stanza further develops the tone, the personality of the speaker, the side of himself that Burns chooses to present:

For me, I swear by sun an' moon,	
And ev'ry star that blinks aboon,	*above*
Ye've cost me twenty pair o' shoon	*shoes*
Just gaun to see you;	*going*
And ev'ry ither pair that's done,	*other*
Mair taen I'm wi' you.	*more taken; with*

The stanza opens with a cliché, swearing by sun and moon. But Burns in the next line undercuts it through ironically rhyming the rustic, slightly oafish "aboon" with moon, and then with the bathetic "shoon" in the following line.

This technique of ironic rhyme, using the rhyme words to point up contrasts or similarities, Burns probably learned from Pope. In this instance, he uses the ironic rhyme to satirize the sublime tradition and to present himself as a poet more at home with poetry about "twenty pair o' shoon" than with poetry about the sun and the moon. When he turns to the subject of poetic theory, then, in the fourth stanza, we

are keyed in to take it seriously but to maintain a certain ironic
distance:

> Just now I've taen the fit o' rhyme,
> My barmie noddle's working prime,   *fermenting*
> My fancy yerket up sublime   *stirred up*
>   Wi' hasty summon:
> Hae ye a leisure-moment's time
> To hear what's comin?
>
>   (ll. 19–24)

Burns goes beyond the praise of spontaneous poetry by placing particular emphasis on the emotions that generate such poetry. He puts
the poem in the immediate present with "Just now" and with the emo-
tive "fit o' rhyme," so that he gives the sense that he is writing without
premeditation, spinning things off just as they come to him. The emphasis on the process of writing is further strengthened by the suggestive words, "barmie," which refers to yeast and its fermenting powers,
and "yerket," a domestic word with implication of "smacking," "beat-
ing," "rousing." His mind is in a creative ferment. The association of
spontaneous writing with momentary sensation runs through the entire
poem, with phrases such as, "I rhyme for fun," "I rhyme away," he has
a *"random shot / O'* countra wit."

When a fictional critic says that Burns is inferior to more learned
poets, " 'There's ither Poets, much your betters, / 'Far seen in *Greek,*
deep men o' *letters,*" Burns does not argue with the pedant. He simply
offers the alternative to himself of the personal freedom that comes
from writing unlettered poetry:

> Then farewel hopes of Laurel-boughs,
> To garland my poetic brows!
> Henceforth, I'll rove where busy ploughs
>   Are whistling thrang,   *busily*
> An' teach the lanely heights an' howes   *hollows*
>   My rustic sang.
>
>   (ll. 49–54)

When he describes the traditional route of the successful poet, which
he is giving up, he uses the diction of the English sublime tradition.
He bids "farewell" to "Laurel-boughs," relinquishes the hope "To gar-
land" his "poetic brows." In lines three to six, when he describes the

alternative, he makes the tone informal through his use of homey imagery, the "busy ploughs" (ironically rhymed with "boughs" and
"brows"), and his mixture of simple English words and rustic-sounding
Scottish words.

In this epistle, also, Burns unfortunately slips into fashionable sentimentality, this time echoing Shenstone (Elegy 21):

> This life, sae far's I understand,
> Is a' enchanted fairy-land,
> Where Pleasure is the Magic-wand,
>   That, wielded right,
> Maks Hours like Minutes, hand in hand,
>   Dance by fu' light.
>
> (ll. 66–72)

Burns seems to have lost his common sense. Pleasure can make hours
dance like minutes, but it will not turn all of life into an "enchanted
fairy land." These occasional forays into the modish poetry of his time
are flaws in his epistles. But they give us the opportunity to see how
Burns transforms these tired and unconvincing ideas into solid experience. He is dull when he is merely imitative of contemporary English
poets like Shenstone, Thomson, and Gray. He is wonderfully alive
when he translates their ideas into his particular combination of the
Standard Habbie verse form, the conversational Scottish style diction,
and his own brand of concreteness:

> Alas! what bitter toil an' straining-
> But truce with peevish poor complaining!
> Is Fortune's fickle *Luna* waning?
>   E'en let her gang!   *go*
> Beneath what light she has remaining,
>   Let's sing our Sang.
>
> (ll. 115–20)

The present reward, singing beneath a fickle, fading moon, maintains
the mixture of pleasure and hardship that regularly comes from defiance of conventional demands. The slightly impatient "But truce," the
short, dismissive line, "E'en let her gang," and the rhyme of "gang"
and "sang" carry through the emphasis on immediate emotions, its
association with writing poetry and unconstrained movement. For-

tune's moon gives only a little light, but it is enough to let us sing our song.

Burns employs the concrete, down-to-earth imagery of peasant food to expand the discussion of everyday hardship. A lot of nonsense had been written in the eighteenth century about the desirability of peasant food, as an example of noble poverty. Burns is the first to treat the subject with realistic acceptance. He gives up the "dreeping roasts" of "countra lairds" and accepts a different way of life:

> 'While ye are pleas'd to keep me hale,
> 'I'll sit down o'er my scanty meal,
> 'Be't *water-brose,* or *muslin-kail,*   *meal and water; vegetable broth*
>   'Wi chearfu' face,
> 'As lang's the Muses dinna fail
>   'To say the grace.'
>   (ll. 139—44)

He does not say that meal and water are preferable to a dripping roast. His meal is "scanty." But he emphasizes the humble parts of life by the use of the specific Scottish peasant terms for these dishes. And he says that dining on *"water-brose"* and *"muslin-kail"* can be joyous when accompanied by health, good cheer, creativity, and grace.

This joy in the details of Scottish life is the form of Scottish nationalism that Burns expresses most often. Just as he prefers individual freedom to the politics of social reform, so he prefers Scottish ordinary life to the politics of Scottish nationalism. It is the everyday life, not the political one, that Burns chooses to dignify.

The misfortunes that are part of his life and, he implies, part of the life of anyone who is not "tideless-blooded, calm and cool," who does not "live by rule," return again and again throughout the poem. But when misfortune appears, Burns confronts it with joy, freedom and poetry:

> An anxious e'e I never throws
> Behint my lug, or by my nose;   *ear*
> I jouk beneath Misfortune's blows   *duck*
>   As weel's I may;
> Sworn foe to *sorrow, care,* and *prose,*
>   I rhyme away.

He can duck beneath "Misfortune's blows . . . as weel's I may" and joke about them by rhyming "nose," "blows," and "prose." To "rhyme away" in poetry and life is the best alternative. Misfortune cannot be denied by a lot of sentimental abstractions, such as calling life an "enchanted fairy land," but it can be dealt with through ducking, joking, and rhyming.

In all the epistles the informal tone, the vernacular diction, the frequent references to ordinary peasant life, and the fluid verse form create a style that is appropriate to a way of life that is free from repressive rules. But the style of the epistles tempers the theme. The ironic rhymes, the consistent images, the varied but regular stanza form, the controlled variation between abstraction and concreteness, the careful intertwining of life's hardship and rewards imply a degree of order. He is not advocating personal or literary anarchy.

In a matter of some eight or nine months, Burns progressed from "Epistle to Davie," which floundered in the abstract ideas and styles of his English contemporaries, to the rich concreteness of "Epistle to J.S****." He stayed in the tradition of benevolism, but translated it, through the use of Scottish eighteenth-century literary traditions, through a judicious choice of the most appropriate English devices, and through his unique sense of concrete, commonplace imagery into a rich expression of the hardships and the possibilities available in a world in which experience is our greatest resource.

The Religious Satires

Many of Burns's satires are directed against the Presbyterian Church—its doctrine of predestination, its evangelical excesses, and the hypocrisy of some of its adherents. Burns explicitly states his reasons for singling out the church, both in his letters and in the satires themselves: anger at the local evangelicals for their treatment of his friend, Gavin Hamilton; personal inclination toward Deism, benevolism, universalism, and other ideas of the Enlightenment that went counter to much of Calvinist teaching; personal opposition to the repressiveness of the church; and the vitriolic dispute between the Evangelicals, the "Auld Lichts," and the Moderates, the "New Lichts," in which he sided with the Moderates.

Burns's satires, especially the early works, tended toward an English Augustan style. Burns had read Pope's satire and invokes him as a model: "O Pope, had I thy satire's darts / To gie [give] the rascals their deserts /

I'd rip their rotten, hollow hearts" ("To the Rev. John M'Math," K 68). The passage takes an unequivocal moral position, a characteristic of much of satire. Maynard Mack, in an influential essay on satire, has said, "Satire . . . asserts the validity and necessity of norms, systematic values, and meanings that *are* contained by recognizable codes. . . . Evil and good are clearly distinguishable . . . and standards of judgment are indubitable."[5] In his earlier satires, such as "Address to the Unco Guid, or the Rigidly Righteous," "The Holy Tulzie," "Holy Willie's Prayer," and "Epitaph on Holy Willie," Burns takes a definable moral stand and clearly distinguishes evil from good. Later in the year 1785, however, his satires, such as "The Holy Fair" and "Address to the Deil" begin to blur the previously clear moral distinctions.

"Holy Willie's Prayer" (K 53), the best of his early religious satires, was written in early 1785 but was not published in the Kilmarnock Edition. Only three religious satires were: "The Holy Fair," "Address to the Deil," and "A Dedication." Burns's suppression of the other poems was probably due to his fear of reprisal from church authorities, who might have banned the book.[6] Later, he published some other satires in the editions of 1787 and 1793. But he never published "Holy Willie's Prayer." The satirical severity of this poem, one of his earliest, was most likely the reason. It was published after Burns's death.

"Holy Willie's Prayer," at the obvious level, is a criticism of hypocrisy, using Holy Willie as an exemplar. (Holy Willie was William Fisher, an ardent Evangelical and an elder of the parish that censured Burns's friend, Gavin Hamilton, for neglect of public worship.) Willie claims to be "a pillar o' thy temple / Strong as a rock," but is actually a fornicator, a drunkard, a man filled with pride, anger, and greed. Equally, the satire is directed against the orthodox Calvinist doctrine of predestination:

> O Thou that in the heavens does dwell!
> Wha, as it pleases best thysel,
> Sends ane to heaven and ten to h——ll,   *one*
>   A' for thy glory!
> And no for ony gude or ill   *good*
>   They've done before thee.
>
>   (ll. 1–6)

Burns satirically portrays Willie as a sophistical wheedler. Willie praises God for five stanzas (ll. 1–30), then slips in the "But yet—O

Lord—confess I must" (l. 36).[7] He follows with a long list of his recent transgressions, with some excuse for each one. Indeed, Willie reveals himself as worse than the people to whom he feels morally superior because he further commits the sins of dishonesty and hypocrisy:

> O L——d—yestreen—thou kens—wi' Meg—   *yesterday*
> Thy pardon I sincerely beg!
> O may't ne'er be a living plague,
>   To my dishonor!
> And I'll ne'er lift a lawless leg
>   Again upon her.
>   (ll. 42–47)

Christianity, for Willie, is a source of weakness rather than strength because he uses the doctrine of Original Sin to excuse his transgressions: "But thou remembers we are dust, / Defil'd wi' sin." And he argues that God has sent him his lust in order to keep him from excessive pride, but that he will humbly bear his burden of a raging libido:

> Maybe thou lets this fleshly thorn
> Buffet thy servant e'en and morn,
> Lest he o'er proud and high should turn,
>   That he's sae gifted;   *so*
> If sae, thy hand maun e'en be borne   *must*
>   Untill thou lift it.
>   (ll. 55–60)

Willie's misuse of the Bible in this stanza further demonstrates the corruption of his soul. He quotes—or misquotes—2 Corinthians 12, "And lest I should be exalted above measure through the abundance of the revelations, there was given to me a thorn in the flesh, the messenger of Satan to buffet me," conveniently leaving out the phrase, "abundance of the revelations." The omitted words express the true intent of the passage—Paul's prayer for humility in the light of Christ's revelation to him. Willie twists the phrase to make it an excuse for his lust—equating the presence of Christ with his desire for wenches.

Willie's lust is exceeded only by his anger, described, characteristically for Burns, in terms of physical sensation. Willie is damning Aiken, who had successfully represented Hamilton in the ecclesiastical court: "My very heart and flesh are quaking / To think how I sat, sweating, shaking, / And p——ss'd wi' dread" (ll. 86–88). And then, in an orgy of anger and vindictiveness:

> L——d, in thy day o' vengeance try him!
> L——d visit him that did employ him!
> And pass not in thy mercy by them,
>   Nor hear their prayer;
> But for thy people's sake destroy them,
>   And dinna spare.   *do not*
>   (ll. 91–96)

Note Burns's use of the short line for the aside, to express Willie's offhanded lack of charity. He urges God, in afterthoughts, to refuse to hear someone's prayer and "dinna spare."

And Willie adds greed to his other sins:

> But L——d, remember me and mine
> Wi' mercies temporal and divine!
> That I for grace and gear may shine,   *wealth*
>   Excell'd by nane!
> And a' the glory shall be thine!
>   Amen! Amen!

The Calvinist belief that God will demonstrate his approval of the Elect leads Willie to a gross materialism that equates God's "grace" with earthly "gear." Burns emphasizes Willie's equation of the two blessings by choosing words that alliterate, have equal length, and equal stress, so that Willie appears to give the same value to God's presence as to his own bank account.

The Calvinist doctrine of predestination is not a theological issue that touches most of us today. But great satire goes beyond its specific subjects to probe the universal moral problems beneath them, to examine the more general human characteristics that cause these problems to occur, and to reveal the universal danger of these errors. Burns has, in "Holy Willie's Prayer," presented the doctrine of predestination as an example of the much more general error of moral arrogance. And he demonstrates the ways in which such arrogance dehumanizes the sinner.

William forces his sexual desire into a pattern consistent with his belief in himself as one of God's chosen. He believes that he is above

sexual desire and that his sensations to the contrary are exceptions, to
be excused by drunkenness or to be regarded as trials sent by God. To
maintain this absurd belief, he separates himself from his feelings, describing his sexual acts in ridiculously mechanical terms, "lift a lawless
leg," "three times—I trow." He inadvertently reveals that his sexual
drive is unending: "Maybe thou lets this fleshly thorn / Buffet thy
servant e'en and morn," and "if sae, thou hand maun [must] e'en be
borne / Untill thou lift it." He is controlled by the sexual drive he
tries to deny, and he becomes incapable of using it for either an expression of love or a source of pleasure. His talk of sex is devoid of tenderness or passion, only a description of a drunken, mindless, joyless
debauch.

His anger is intensified by his self-importance. He is not content
just to be angry at Hamilton and Aiken, he needs to enlist God as his
ally. The curse he lays on Gavin Hamilton, "Curse thou his basket and
his store, / Kail and potatoes," is a quotation from Deuteronomy 28,
"Cursed shall be thy basket and thy store." In the biblical context, the
curse is laid on those who "wilt not hearken unto the voice of the Lord
thy God." Willie's high opinion of himself causes him to see himself
as almost God's equal. As his anger proceeds from stanza to stanza, it
becomes a vindictive rage, "But for thy people's sake destroy them, /
And dinna [don't] spare." He becomes overwhelmed and controlled by
his emotions, driven by lust, consumed by hate and greed, and finally
blinded by vanity ("Excell'd by nane").

Burns makes Willie look as ridiculous as he deserves. A man who
condemns everyone's fornication but his own, who wants God's curse
to extend to his enemy's "Kail and potatoes," is an absurd monster who
deserves to be laughed at. But Burns goes beyond Willie's ridiculous-
ness to demonstrate the destruction of his own vitality. Willie's self-
satisfaction turns sexual drives to emotionless lust, anger to sterile
rage, and desire for grace to narrow materialism. Willie's arrogance
stems from his orthodox Calvinism. But if we try to deny our human
weaknesses we will look as ridiculous as Willie and will be as destruc-
tive of our own humanity.

Burns takes no position on the specifically Calvinist condemnation
of lust, anger, and greed. We can read this poem either as an argument
for obedience to Christian principles or for their relaxation. But in his
denunciation of self-satisfaction and pride, Burns is in the older Augustan satiric tradition. He takes a clear moral stance and implies an
alternative, that we must acknowledge our moral limitations and try

to live with them. After "Holy Willie's Prayer" Burns moved further from the Augustan style of satire.

Burns wrote "The Holy Fair" (K 70) several months after "Holy Willie's Prayer" and probably revised it some months later, early in 1786. In that period his anger seems generally to have abated, and most of his satires take a milder, more detached stance. The moral rigor that he showed in "Holy Willie's Prayer" mellowed. Possibly some of the change was due to his state of mind—his letters of the period begin to show less anger. But part of it also was the influence of current ideas.

Benevolism, in particular, seems to have influenced Burns in the same way that it was influencing some of his English contemporaries or near contemporaries, such as Gray, Goldsmith, and Shenstone. The English satirists, such as Churchill, Anstey, and Robert Lloyd, however, were still strongly influenced by Pope's satire and tended to deviate only slightly from his style, even when their ideas were different. Burns, along with the English satirists, used models from Pope. But he had, in addition, a resource lacking to English writers, the various Scottish forms of satire. In "The Holy Fair" he merges Scottish and English styles to create a new kind of satire.

The form he uses is strictly Scottish, going back to the Middle Ages. Two older works in the form, *Peblis to the Play* and *Chrystis Kirk of the Grene,* were possibly known to Burns. Burns particularly used as a model two poems by Robert Fergusson in this genre, *Hallow-Fair* and *Leith Races.*

The verse form is one that is always used in this type of poem, with some variations. The alternating iambic tetrameter and iambic trimeter lines are common to most examples, as is the repeating final word. The rhyme scheme, *a b a b c d c d e,* and the final dimeter line come from Fergusson's *Leith Races.* Also from Fergusson is the style of loose pattern of rhyme, with frequent oblique rhymes, some instances of assonance instead of rhyme (e.g., ll. 51 and 53), and some instances of internal rhyme instead of end rhyme (e.g., ll. 68 and 70).

The form describes a public, rowdy event, frequented by farmers, laborers, and servants, described in an informal style and in a comic, light-hearted tone. The form is sometimes called a "brawl." The speaker keeps shifting the focus to describe various activities and to emphasize inconsistencies. It is a full-bodied, lusty form, which describes, accepts, and rarely condemns. The poem usually describes an actual event, and Burns almost certainly had in mind the Mauchline

Fair, which had occurred around the time he wrote the first draft of this poem. Contemporary prose descriptions of the Mauchline Fair indicate that it was very much as he has described it.

Burns combines the easy toleration of the Scottish form with Pope's style of sharp contrasts and ironic rhyme to satirize Presbyterian preaching. By combining the two approaches, he brilliantly creates a new form that contrasts life as it really is against the pretenses of the church. James Kinsley says, "He opposes the force of sexual and social instinct to the shams of pulpit rhetoric and 'polemical divinity'; and he builds these oppositions up out of the sustained irony of worship, drink, and fornication juxtaposed."[8] I think that Kinsley is right, but the poem goes further than he says.

The opening of the poem, like its model, *Leith Races,* has a lovely description of fresh, unspoiled nature that, it could be argued, sets off the rowdiness and hypocrisy of the center of the poem. If this was Burns's intent, he unfortunately does not develop it, because the setting does not recur and is easily forgotten in the body of the poem. Burns also introduces, in the opening stanzas, three "hizzies": Fun, Supersition, and Hypocrisy, following Fergusson's allegory of Mirth. Again, the poetic possibilities are there but unrealized, for Burns seems to forget these allegories as well. It seems that Burns followed Fergusson rather uncritically in the first six stanzas.

It is only at stanza 7 that the poem becomes truly original. From here to the conclusion it alternates between descriptions of the enormous variety of people, actions, and events, and description of the preaching. Burns starts with a description of ordinary Scottish life such as is typical of Scottish literature, but which he accomplishes with very special success:

Here, farmers gash, in ridin graith,	*respectable; habit*
Gaed hoddan by their cotters;	*go jogging; tenants*
There, swankies young, in braw braid-claith,	*strapping lads; good broadcloth*
Are springin owre the gutters.	*over*
The lasses, skelpin barefit thrang,	*skipping; crowd*
In silks and scarlet glitter;	
Wi' *sweet-milk cheese,* in mony a whang,	*thick slice*
An' *farls,* bak'd wi' butter,	*small cakes*
Fu' crump that day.	*crisp*

Burns soon turns to satiric treatment of his subject, combining the Scottish technique of rapidly shifting scenes with Pope's technique of contrasts, ironic rhymes, and use of one verb to govern contrasting objects:

> Here, some are thinkan on their sins,
>   An' some upo' their claes;   *clothes*
> Ane curses feet that fyl'd his shins,   *defiled*
>   Anither sighs an' pray's.
>   (ll. 82–85)

The contrasting subjects, emphasized by the use of the verb "thinkan" to govern both sins and clothes and by the rhymes of "sins" with "shins" and "claes" with "pray's," contribute to the satiric treatment of the scene. Hypocrisy is not the subject because the same person does not think about sins and clothes. Burns's satire is directed against the desire for a universal moral standard, which he argues is impossible, rather than against the inconsistency in the behavior of any one individual.

When the preaching starts, the variety increases. One Evangelical preacher is described:

> Hear how he clears the points o' Faith
>   Wi' rattlin an' thumpin!
> Now meekly calm, now wild in wrath,
>   He's stampan, an' he' jumpan!
> His lengthen'd chin, his turn'd up snout,
>   His eldritch squeel and gestures,   *unearthly*
> O how they fire the heart devout,
>   Like cantharidian plaisters
>   On sic a day!
>   (ll. 109–17)

Burns changes the diction to indicate a shift in speaker. The first and third lines of this stanza are in the grandiloquent, pulpit rhetoric of a pretentious preacher. The second and fourth lines are in the diction of an innocent, impressionable, slightly awestruck peasant. The preacher and the peasant both appear slightly ridiculous. The "cantharidian plaisters" in the eighth line were believed to be aphrodisiacs, a form of Spanish fly. So Burns now combines the themes of sexual activities and religious emotions, which have both been running through the poem, to suggest that the "heart devout" may be fired for at least two reasons. The stanza, then, mixes two points of view and two kinds of devout

hearts to establish the moral confusion that governs the remainder of
the poem.

The Fair then breaks into religious turmoil. The *"real judges . . .
canna sit for anger."* A "New Licht" preacher bores with his "cauld
harangues" so that the godly go off to "gie the jars an' barrels / A lift
that day." This Moderate, who preaches like "some auld pagan
heathen" with "ne'er a word o' *faith,"* is countered by an "Auld Licht,"
who sends Common-Sense up the road. The Evangelical/Moderate dispute is revealed as one more futile distinction, a choice between giving
up faith or giving up common sense. After this dispute, the chaos is
everywhere.

The change house fills with commentators calling for food and drink
and logic and scripture. "They raise a din, that, in the end, / Is like
to breed a rupture." The moral confusion increases as the "lads and
lasses" "mind baith *soul* an' *body."* The preaching becomes increasingly
emotional, described in the effect it has on the listener physically, "His
piercin words, like Highlan swords, / Divide the joints and marrow."
Hell is described:

> A vast, unbottom'd, boundless *Pit,*
> > Fill'd fou a' *lowan brunstane,*   *full of; flaming brimstone*
> Whase raging flame, an' scorching heat,
> > Whad melt the hardest whunstane!   *would; hard rock*
> > > (ll. 190–94)

Burns undercuts the infernal rhetoric with an abrupt return to reality,
" 'Twas but some neebor *snoran* / Asleep that day."

The preaching without faith, without common sense, without conviction ("Tho in his heart he weel believes / An' thinks it auld wives
fables," ll. 147–48) and the indiscriminate mixture of preaching with
all the ordinary activities—eating, drinking, sleeping, flirting—provide an analogue of moral chaos in which nothing seems to make much
sense or to show much order.

The confluence of sex and religion becomes complete in the last two
stanzas, as the participants begin to stagger home:

> At slaps the billies halt a blink,   *fence openings; lads; moment*
> > Till lasses strip their shoon   *take off; shoes*
> Wi' *faith* an' *hope,* an' *love* an' *drink,*
> > They're a' in famous tune
> > > For crack that day.   *talking*
> > > (ll. 230–35)

The biblical "faith, hope, and love" are altered by the "drink." Each word of the traditional virtues takes on a different meaning. The young people's faith and hope is that the flirtations will result in lovemaking; and "love" becomes a euphemism for sex. Yet the quotation retains some of its religious implications. The moral ambiguity increases in the last part of the final stanza:

> There's some are fou o' *love divine*;
> There's some are fou o' *brandy*;
> An' monie jobs that day begin,
> May end in *Houghmagandie*   *fornication*
> Some ither day.
> (ll. 239–44)

The "love divine" can apply to those moved to religious zeal and to the sexually aroused young men and women. Burns has blurred distinctions. He points out, with amused detachment, the way in which religion and sexuality can so easily become enmeshed.

The structure of the poem has partly been, as Kinsley says, based on the contrast between natural forces and sham rhetorical preaching. But the satiric statement of the poem is, finally, more complex because the contrast is less vivid. Looked at one way, almost everyone is shamming. Looked at another way, almost everyone is sincere. Except for the preacher in stanza 17, there are no rank hypocrites in the poem. However foolish the preachers may look, they seem to mean what they are saying. The young people, for the most part, did not come to the Holy Fair pretending virtue but seeking sex. They were not exactly clear what their purpose was. Everyone looks a bit foolish but few are clearly reprehensible.

In presenting so many moral ambiguities, in alluding to the Bible so equivocally, in constantly shifting the point of view and the diction, in describing so wide a variety of human behavior, and in creating a broad analogue of chaos, Burns is saying that rigorous moral distinctions simply have little bearing on life's experience. The preaching filled some people with "love divine" in the godly sense. It also made others sexually excited. And natural drives inevitably assert themselves, so that sexual drive becomes similar to the rush for food and drink and to the snoring that sounded like Hell.

Burns has daringly taken the benevolist doctrine to its richest, most inescapable conclusion, saying that most human behavior is morally acceptable. Most people, Burns says, behave in ways that are a bit ridiculous, but few are steeped in sin. The natural drives must be accepted because they are pervasive and inevitable.

And he has developed the Scottish form beyond any of its past realizations by combining this interesting but previously undistinguished kind of poem with the techniques of Pope, the ideas of the Enlightenment, and his own benign point of view. He has, indeed, used the form of the peasant "brawl" to create a new kind of satire, one that uses the chaos of activity to provide an analogue for a moral brawl. In this form, the satire no longer insists on a clear distinction between good and evil. Few people, Burns says, pretend to behave in one way and act in another. Most people do something in between. Abstract moral distinctions can be and usually are more rigid than is consistent with the way people behave or need to behave. Burns rejects the orthodox notion of Original Sin. We ought not, he says, have unrealistic moral expectations of ourselves or of others.

"The Holy Fair" is a superb example of a poem that balances the firm moral position of Augustan satire (and "Holy Willie's Prayer") with the tolerant acceptance of benevolism. It is probably the greatest satire to express the benevolist idea. But in "Address to the Deil" (K 76) Burns goes still further toward creating a new mode.

In "Address to the Deil" Burns uses a familiar subject to express the complex, human conflict between reason and religion in the late eighteenth century. The poem is not philosophical and does not explore the intellectual issues involved in that conflict. Rather, it describes the way the conflict must have been experienced in ordinary, day-to-day life. The mode is comic and satiric, which allows Burns a certain detachment. But beneath the jocular tone Burns eloquently expresses the perplexity.

The Devil, obviously, had long been a topic of interest for Christianity, but he had become especially important to orthodox Calvinism because of its preoccupation with sin. In Scotland, as in other rural parts of Europe, interest in Satan combined with local superstitions, some of them pre-Christian, to provide an elaborate, popular complex of beliefs. In Burns's Scotland, the Devil and associated belief in superstition existed in a wide range of popular and theological beliefs. Belief in witches as agents of the Devil, for example, a belief especially familiar in the history of American Calvinism, existed in parts of Scotland.

Belief in the Devil and in superstition ran strongly counter to most ideas of the Enlightenment. Some of the advocates of the Enlightenment were Christians, and most of the others found a mild form of Christianity tolerable. But they vigorously opposed those parts of religion or popular belief that concentrated on the dark, irrational, unknowable part of human experience. Belief in the Devil and in the superstition related to him was an idea the Enlightenment hoped to erase.

Burns's own attitude toward Satan, human evil, and the unknowable, irrational part of the world is ambivalent. At times he hailed Milton's Satan as his "favorite hero" (R 113), seeing him, as others did in the late eighteenth century, as a symbol of proud rebellion against unreasonable authority. In his prose, Burns never contradicts this view, but he qualifies it.

In spite of his benevolist tendencies, Burns does not completely dismiss the idea of Original Sin or the idea of a Devil dwelling inside us. When he expresses benevolist ideas he still refrains from seeing man as essentially virtuous. For example, he writes, with complicated qualifications, "Every man even the worst, have something good about them, though very often nothing else than a happy temperament of constitution inclining them to this or that virtue" (CB, 7). And his attitude toward superstition is explicitly ambivalent. In his autobiographical letter (R 125) he says: "I owed much to an old Maid of my Mother's, remarkable for her ignorance, credulity and superstition.— She had, I suppose, the largest collection in the county of tales and songs concerning devils, ghosts. . . . [This] had so strong an effect on my imagination, that to this hour, in my nocturnal rambles, I sometimes keep a sharp look-out in suspicious places; and though nobody can be more sceptical in these matters than I, yet it often takes an effort of Philosophy to shake off these idle terrors." His statement that he is both sceptical and must shake off idle terrors aptly summarizes his personal ambivalence: the conflict between mental and visceral responses to evil and to the supernatural that infuses his poetry.

Running in and out of Burns's works is a desire both to agree with and to question the Enlightenment thinkers' reliance on reason. He was attracted, as were so many people of his period, to the clear thinking of the Enlightenment and to its promise of intellectual and personal freedom from the authority of church and state. But he also believed that much about human psychology was left unexplained by the benign theories of some Enlightenment thinkers. He recognized that Christianity held certain profound truths. The concept of the Devil provided a metaphor for some of them, in particular the ideas that

man is not always as good as benevolism would make him and that
much of the world seems capricious, beyond correction or control.

In "Address to the Deil" he has used the idea of the Devil to bring
these conflicting yet conterminous ideas together, both mocking and
accepting the Devil, moving in and out of belief by carefully controlling the poem's point of view and tone. Through this variation of style,
he makes a statement, one of the earliest in European literature, that
the old beliefs have great limitations but we do not know enough about
the physical world or human psychology to give these beliefs up entirely. He expresses, with truly poetic suggestiveness, the combination
of befuddled scepticism and dubious faith that has characterized much
of Western thinking in the past two centuries.

In the first stanza, Burns sets the tone by varying the diction, shifting from pretentious pulpit rhetoric in pure English to down-to-earth
colloquialisms in a mixture of English and Scots:

> O Thou, whatever title suit thee!
> Auld Hornie, Satan, Nick, or Clootie,   *cloven-footed*
> Wha in yon cavern grim an' sooty
>   Clos'd under hatches,
> Spairges about the brunstane cootie,   *splashes; brimstone; basin*
>   To scaud poor wretches!   *scald*

The shift to familiar, even intimate terms (with the diminutive "Cloo-
tie") and the description of Satan splashing about in a huge brimstone
wash basin reveal Burns's familiarity with the Devil, someone he can
joke about or poke mild fun at. Burns is not awed by the Devil, but
neither does he dismiss him.

In stanza four Burns combines several interpretations of the Devil:

> Whyles, ranging like a roaring lion,   *sometimes*
> For prey, a' holes an' corners tryin;   *all*
> Whyles, on the strong-wing'd Tempest flyin,
>   Tirlan the *kirks*;   *stripping; churches*
> Whyles, in the human bosom pryin,
>   Unseen thou lurks.

The first line is a striaghforward biblical description of the Devil
(1 Peter 5); the third line refers to the common superstition that Satan
rides the storms; and the fifth and sixth lines are psychological, ac-

cepting the doctrine of Original Sin, that the Devil lurks "unseen" in human bosoms. The Devil becomes a symbol that includes the Bible, popular superstition, traditional Christianity, and human psychology.

Some stanzas seem to accept superstitions and their connection with the Devil. Burns accepts the beliefs of his "rev'rend *Graunie*," a "douse, [gentle, sober] honest, woman," so that the stanzas from line 49 to line 72 become straightforward descriptions of superstitions and the Devil's work.[9] But other stanzas present the Devil as a product of naive or drunken imagination. Lines 37–42 describe what Burns pretends is his own point of view, jokingly assuming the role of a credulous, oafish peasant, who is sure he has seen the Devil. Then:

> The cudgel in my nieve did shake,   *fist*
> Each bristl'd hair stood like a stake,
> When wi' an eldritch, stoor *quaik, quaik,*   *unearthly; harsh*
>   Amang the springs,
> Awa ye squatter'd like a *drake,*   *fluttered*
>   On whistling wings.

The vivid description of the speaker's physical reactions and the amusing rhyme of "shake," "stake," and "quaik" undermine the frightened speaker who believes, for no apparent reason, that a drake is the Devil. In lines 73–78 a drunk follows a will-o'-the-wisp to his death, for which Burns ironically blames the Devil.

The subtle alternation between probable and imaginary events establishes the point of view of the poem. We cannot be sure whether the Devil interferes in our lives or whether we imagine him. And the poet has maintained an ironic, teasing distance, satirizing credulity at one moment, accepting popular superstitions at another. Having established this elusive, suggestive stance, he moves on to the Devil in the Bible.

In lines 85–108 he comments on two biblical tales of Satan, the seduction of Adam and Eve and the temptation of Job. Eden before the Fall is described mostly in elevated, affected English, "Sweet on the fragrant, flow'ry swaird, / In shady bow'r," a diction appropriate to a mythological world.[10] When we turn to daily life, the way it is since the loss of Eden, the diction becomes earthy, with many Scotticisms and expressions of strong emotion, mostly rustic anger. The Devil is an "auld, snickdrawing [sneaky] dog," the Fall of Man and its aftermath is described, "An' gied [gave] the infant warld a shog [shake

up], / 'Maist [almost] ruin'd a'." The description of the ills Satan visited on Job are listed, with "An' lows'd [loosed] his ill-tongued,
wicked *Scawl* [scold] / Was warst ava." Burns relates those two familiar
stories in terms of immediate emotions and experience. They tell about
events, he implies, as alive for him and for most people as any current
happening. The presence of the Devil, creating evil and tempting us,
is far too entwined with our experience, too immediate and energetic,
to be dismissed for some abstract reason.

In the penultimate stanza Burns turns to himself, still in familiar
diction, but without the previous oafish credulity. The Devil is an
intimate, "Auld *Cloots*," and a psychological force. He influences
Burns's behavior, not, superstitiously, his milk or his loom (ll. 55–
66). He is, however, only an influence. Burns has free choice:

> An' now, auld *Cloots*, I ken ye're thinkan,
> A certain *Bardie's*, rantin, drinkin,
> Some luckless hour will send him linkan,   *bounding*
>   To your black pit;
> But faith! he'll turn a corner jinkan,   *darting*
>   An' cheat you yet.

Burns's acceptance of his own responsibility has a twofold implication. It denies the Calvinist doctrine of predestination because Burns
has control over his own destiny and his own hope for salvation. But
it also accepts the idea of the Devil as a part of human psychology, as
a motive in behavior. Burns, with beautiful irony, does not deny his
own sinful behavior, "A certain *Bardie's* rantin, drinkin," nor does he
deny the possibility of his own damnation, "Some luckless hour will
send him linkan, / To your black pit." But he tentatively expects,
without total conviction, to outsmart the Devil, which means that he
hopes to overcome his own irresponsible tendencies, "But faith! he'll
turn a corner jinkan, / An' cheat you yet." Burns rejects the benevolist
doctrine that we have no Devil in us. But he also rejects the Calvinist
doctrine that we have no control over that Devil.

The ultimate challenge to predestination comes in the final stanza:

> But fare you weel, auld *Nickie-ben*!
> O wad ye tak a thought an' men'!   *would; and mend*
> Ye aiblins might—I dinna ken—   *perhaps; don't know*

> Still hae a *stake*—
> I'm wae to think upo' yon den,   *woeful*
> Ev'n for your sake.

This stanza profoundly challenges Calvinist predestination by saying that even the Devil can have free will and be saved. The notion is not new with Burns. But Burns's personal concern for the Devil brings the idea into a new sensibility. Burns "wae" in thinking about "yon den," in this atmosphere of camaraderie with the Devil, is of a piece with the familiarity of the descriptions of the biblical stories. The concept of Hell and the Devil—the evil within us, superstition, punishment— is part of Burns's everyday thoughts. The sense of immediacy, the concentration on his momentary sensations are here translated into a refutation of the rationalistic arguments of the Enlightenment. Hell is real because Burns feels it to be real.

The poem has at once affirmed and denied the existence of the Devil. It has seen him as a figure to be feared and to be joked about, as a product of common experience and of drunken imagination. The tentativeness of the final stanza, "I dinna ken," makes the hope of the Devil's reformation and Burns's concern for him consonant with the tentativeness of the rest of the poem. We cannot know even if the Devil will be with us forever. Maybe Burns can "turn a corner jinkan." Maybe the Devil can. In either case, Burns must still, in the present, think about "you den" and about the wretches who will get scalded by the boiling water Satan splashes on them out of his enormous brimstone wash basin.

"Address to the Deil" is a brilliant satire on both orthodox Calvinism—its obsession with evil, its arrogant denial of free will—and of the Enlightenment—its premature confidence, its arrogant certainty in the primacy of reason. But Burns has transcended the form of satire to create a new form, one that denies all the certainty that conventional satire was built on. The "norms, systematic values, . . . recognizable codes" are gone. He has achieved a complete turnabout by satirizing the very certainty satire had assumed. He has progressed, in a matter of a few months, from the conventional "Holy Willie's Prayer" to the creation of a new form. It is a form more appropriate than traditional satire for the age of uncertainty that began in Burns's time and has continued until our own. He was one of the first to recognize this age and to articulate its problems.

Other Satiric Works

Burns directs some of his other satires toward the inadequacies of the social system in a way comparable to the reconsideration of religion in the religious satires. He describes and evaluates class structure, conventional manners, fashions, sexual morality, and traditional restraints on behavior and offers some alternatives.

Burns has structured "To a Louse, On Seeing one on a Lady's Bonnet at Church" (K 83) around the contrast of pretension and reality. Jennie is sitting in church, impressed by her own fine clothes and unaware that a louse is climbing up her new bonnet. Burns, with apparent effortlessness, expands the trivial incident into a highly suggestive symbol.

The location in a church provides Burns with the opportunity to deliver a kind of sermon, one derived from observation and experience rather than from the authority of priest, scriptures, or doctrine. As such, the poem might appear to be no more than a parable, a cleverly disguised Deistic sermon "that would probably seem sententious outside this eccentric context. . . . a rival sermon on vanity."[11] Burns, however, has manipulated the point of view of the speaker to make this poem into a satire on the class system and a commentary on the way we see the social world.

The speaker in this poem is a naive, rustic bumpkin. Burns uses Scottish words to convey the sense of a country boy talking, someone without the elegance that Jenny thinks she has. He is truly impressed by the louse, "Ha! whare ye gaun, ye crowlan ferlie [creeping marvel]!" "I canna say but ye strunt [strut] rarely," "Ye ugly, creepan, blastet wonner [damned wonder]," and "Swith [get going], in some beggar's haffet [lock of hair at the temple] squattle [squat, nestle]." Spellings such as "gaun," "crowlan," "creepan" give the sense of an uneducated person speaking. Words like "ferlie," "swith," "squattle," the sort of old-fashioned, racy words spoken by articulate country people, give concreteness and vigor to his speech. Burns, then, establishes his speaker as naive, impressionable, but articulate.

The speaker is apparently taken in by Jenny's pretenses. "How daur ye set your fit upon her, / Sae fine a *Lady!*" And he takes the class system seriously, arguing that the louse should know its place in the social scheme, "In some beggar's haffet squattle" and "Miss's fine *Lunardi,* fye / How daur ye do it." A "Lunardi" was a balloon shaped bonnet, named after a pilot of an early balloon flight. It was the height of fashion in 1785 and, by fortunate coincidence, a symbol of a faddish experiment of the Enlightenment.

At the center of the poem Burns expands Jenny's fancy hat into a comic symbol of the louse's ambition as it rises on the balloon:

> Now haud you there, ye're out o' sight,
> Beneath the fatt'rels, snug and tight,   *ribbon ends*
> Na faith ye yet! ye'll no be right,   *damn you*
>   Till ye've got on it,
> The vera tapmost, towrin height   *topmost; towering*
>   O'Miss's bonnet.

Burns has the impressionable speaker express particular wonder as he gazes higher and higher at the ascending louse, "The vera tapmost, towrin height." As the louse ascends, indifferent to the speaker's increasingly emotional harangue, the absurdity of the speaker's desire to set things right intensifies. Burns uses the short line to give the speaker's voice an additional slam:

> O for some rank, mercurial rozet   *resin*
>   Or fell, red smeddum   *harsh, red vermin killer*
> I'd gie you sic a hearty dose o't,
>   Wad dress your droddum!   *whip your ass*

In the penultimate stanza the speaker advises Jenny:

> O *Jenny* dinna toss your head,   *don't*
> An' set your beauties a' abroad!   *abroad*
> Ye little ken what cursed speed   *understand*
>   The blastie's makin!   *damned thing*
> Thae *winks* and *finger-ends*, I dread   *those*
>   Are notice takin!

His advice to her, not to toss her head, is based on his concern over the louse's speed and the notice of the other congregants, who are winking and pointing their fingers.

The last stanza includes two famous lines:

> O wad some Pow'r the giftie gie us
> *To see oursels as others see us!*
> It wad frae monie a blunder free us

> An' foolish notion:
> What airs in dress an' gait wad lea'e us,
> And ev'n Devotion!

This stanza is the basis for the criticism that the poem becomes sententious, with a nice moral to sum up the situation too neatly for the
earthy context.

But the stanza is more than just a "sermon on vanity." In the context
of the poem, the often-quoted lines also relate to the subtext of the
poem, that the class system is an example of human pretensions. The
belief in a class system and its symbols of elaborate clothing (a form of
symbolism taken even more seriously in the eighteenth century than
in our own) is made to appear absurd. It is as absurd, Burns says, as
Jenny's vanity, because it derives from the human pretensions that say
we can impose order where none exists.

The speaker, for all his belief in the class system, and for all his
oafishness, still sees the absurdity of Jenny's belief in her own social
superiority. Even the louse is indifferent to the distinctions between a
"fine *Lunardi*" and a "beggar's haffet." When an uneducated country
boy sees things more clearly than "Sae fine a *Lady*," when a louse ig-
nores the social symbols, something is wrong with the system. So when
Burns says "To see oursels as others see us" he is referring to more than
the vanity of fancy clothes. He is satirizing the belief that we humans
can impose an arbitrary social order on the complex world of humans.

Burns wrote *Love and Liberty* (K 84), more commonly known as *The
Jolly Beggars,* in 1785 but never published it. He considered including
it in his second edition of poems, the Edinburgh Edition of 1787, but
was dissuaded from doing so by a prominent Edinburgh critic, the
Reverend Hugh Blair, because it was "much too licentious."

As usual, Burns drew from a wide range of sources. For the form,
he drew on various poems about beggars, such as *The Happy Beggars,* a
collection of songs about the joys of the simple life.[12] The "brawl"
poem, which was also a source for "The Holy Fair," had some influence
in the use of commonplace descriptions and shifting focus. *Love and
Liberty* is influenced by John Gay's *The Beggar's Opera,* a satirical drama
about low-life characters who express a range of views commenting on
the values and behavior of the upper and middle classes. For subject
matter, Burns also drew on an actual experience in a local tavern,
Poosie Nansie's, mentioned in the opening recitativo.

The ideas in *Love and Liberty* were influenced by contemporary benevolism, which often idealized the outcasts and saw them as people to observe and learn from. Its title comes from a poem that expresses benevolist ideas, Pope's "Eloisa to Abelard": "O happy state! when souls each other draw, / When love is liberty, and nature law." Pope's poem is in the form of a letter from Eloisa (a medieval woman who was disgraced by a love affair) to her lover, Abelard. Pope depicts her belief in love, liberty, and the law of nature, which is a major theme in Burns's poem. As McGuirk says, "The fierceness with which the beggars articulate their creed and attack the norm seems achieved through Burns's emulation of Pope."[13]

Burns also uses the scene of outcasts from society to represent the fulfillment of a wish that he often expressed, to slip out of society and live free of its constraints: to wander "adrift." In *Love and Liberty* he explores that wish further than he had done in his epistles, developing the implications of his personal wish into a broad commentary on social behavior.[14]

The poem has a repeating theme of political and social criticism. The soldier must "beg, with a wooden arm and leg" and "with hoary locks . . . must stand the winter shocks, / Beneath the woods and rocks oftentimes for a home." The martial chuck was "reduced to beg in despair" by the peace. She describes the army chaplain as a "sanctified *sot*." "He ventured the Soul, and I risked the Body." The Highland widow describes her dead husband as a victim of the oppression of the Highlands by Lowland laws. There are references to "Hunger, Cauld, an' a' sic harms." But the political and social ills are described so that they can be overcome by defiance, assertion, energy, passion. The poem is primarily psychological. It describes the way to live outside the system, not how to change it.

Love and Liberty has four parts. The introduction, which is the first recitativo (ll. 1–28), creates the setting. Then there are two dramatic episodes. The first (ll. 29–80) consists of the songs sung by the soldier and his woman and the brief recitativo between them. The second episode (ll. 81–249) consists of several recitativos and songs that express a complicated interchange among a Highland widow, a pigmy fiddler, a tinker, an anonymous woman, and a poet. The final episode is the concluding hymn (ll. 250–281), in which all join.[15]

The first part describes a harsh storm, which contrasts the cozy, jolly interior of the tavern. The second part, the episode of the soldier and his woman, examines the ways the beggars deal with the injustice of war. The soldier's loss of arm and leg means that, if called, "I'd clatter

on my stumps at the sound of a drum." He still "could meet a troop
of Hell at the sound of a drum." Each stanza ends with "sound of a
drum," emphasized by the music, which has a steady, martial beat,
like the marching drum.[16] The martial chuck has had a varied career
but faces the future with joy. No matter what her problems, she finds
pleasure in recalling her "Sodger laddie": "His leg was so tight and his
cheek was so ruddy." She responded to the drunken sanctimoniousness
of the chaplain by personal assertion, "The Regiment at Large for a
Husband I got." When reduced to begging, she can still find pleasure
in her newest love because his "Rags Regimental they flutter'd so
gaudy." She does not know how long she has lived, but can still join
in drinking and singing, "whilst with both hands I can hold the glass
steady." She will fend off old age as long as she can, just as the soldier
will clatter on his stumps as long as he can.

Neither figure is idealized. The internal rhymes equate the soldier's
various activities that gave him his cuts and scars: "This here was for
a wench, and that other in a trench, / When welcoming the French at
the sound of the drum." The chuck readily admits that she "prov'd
false" to her first love. And after the chaplain, "From the gilded Spon-
toon to the Fife I was ready." But they are both so direct and honest
about their way of life, so obviously prepared to find pleasure where
they can, that they come through as wonderfully admirable.

The second interchange is more complicated. Each song in this episode presents a different aspect of life outside the system, each one
flawed and qualifying the easy acceptance of the first episode. The
Highland widow's state is less satisfactory than that of the two previous
singers. She is full of curses, "must mourn / The Pleasures that will
ne'er return," and her one "comfort" is "a hearty can." The pigmy
fiddler woos the widow, looking slightly ridiculous as he croons, "Wi'
hand on hainch [hips], and upward e'e." He sings a merry song, as-
serting the old Burnsian theme of the simple pleasures that are available to all:

> Sae merrily's the banes we'll pyke,   *pick at*
> An' sun oursells about the dyke;
> An' at our leisure when ye like
>   We'll whistle owre the lave o't.
>   (ll. 141–44)

But his capacity for simple joy does not help him as much as it does
the speaker in the epistles. The tinker, taking the widow away from

him, brutally "swore by a' was swearing worth / To speet him like a Pliver [put him on a spit like a bird]," and he refers to the pigmy as "that Shrimp, that withered Imp." The tinker's victory is described in a satire on courtly love, which contrasts and rhymes the diction of conventional love poetry with the reality of a tavern brawl:

> The Caird prevail'd—th' unblushing fair   *tinker*
>   In his embraces sunk;
> Partly wi' Love o'ercome sae sair.   *so sore*
>   An' partly she was drunk.
>   (ll. 182–84)

The sexual encounters are deromanticized by the widow's easy capitulation to the tinker and by the action of the pigmy—who immediately finds himself another woman—whom he "rak'd . . . Fore and Aft, / Behint the Chicken cavie [coop]." That woman's lover, the Bard, is not bothered because he has two others: "I've lost but Ane, I've Twa behin'."

The Bard then sings about the pleasure of women. Burns uses the familiar Scottish refrain "an a' that" to dismiss both traditional love poetry and the romanticized view of sex that it expresses:

> In raptures sweet this hour we meet,
>   Wi' mutual love an' a' that;
> But for how lang the Flie May Stang   *fly; sting*
>   Let Inclination law that.   *decree*
>   (ll. 224–27)

The Bard has his doubts about women: "Their tricks an' craft hae put me daft [crazy, but also sexually excited]," but still calls to "Clear your decks an' here's the sex! / I like the jads for a' that."

Burns presents a parody of aristocratic courtship and conventional love poetry through the use of elevated diction in the Highland widow's song and elsewhere: "heav'n o' charms," "th' unblushing fair"— note the "unblushing"—and "Their humble slave an' a' that"; and in such terms as the tinker's "roosty rapier," "hurchin [urchin] Cupid," and the "care-defying blade, / As ever Bacchus listed." He is following the pattern of Gay's *Beggar's Opera*, which also has beggars and whores behaving like their social betters. In both works the significance is that the satire of mores works both ways. The bawdy sexuality of the beggars is a mirror image of upper-class morality, only more honest. In this work, however, the manners of courtship are considerably rougher than in *The Beggar's Opera* and signify more than a satire of high society's behavior.

The beggars' defiance, affirmation, and insistent joy in the face of enormous adversity are all admirable. But an undertone reminds us of human limitations. Their actions are often brutal and exploitive. The sexual behavior is undoubtedly more pleasurable than that practiced by Holy Willie, but if exemplified by raking a woman "fore and aft" behind a chicken coop, it is scarcely idealized. Before the concluding hymn the beggars pawn their clothes for drink, "Scarcely left to coor their fuds [cover their tails]." The Bard leads the final hymn "Between his Twa Deborahs."

The concluding hymn is a superb song of defiance of all convention, with a powerful beat to the music that denotes individual and common energy:

> A fig for those by law protected!
>   Liberty's a glorious feast!
> Courts for Cowards were erected,
>   Churches built to please the Priest.
>   (ll. 254–57)

But when the beggars ask: "Does the sober bed of Marriage / Witness brighter scenes of love?" we might be inclined to answer, "Yes." It would not take much for a marriage bed to witness brighter scenes than these in which the tinker brutalizes his rival, the pigmy has mindless sex behind a chicken coop, and the Bard readily gives up his mistress because he has two more. The beggars go on to sing:

> Life is all a Variorum,
>   We regard not how it goes;
> Let them cant about Decorum,
>   Who have character to lose.
>   (ll. 270–73)

The beggars cannot "cant about decorum" in their situation because they have no characters to lose. Their absence of character does grant them considerable freedom, but it also takes a certain toll.

Most of us have at some time shared Burns's wish to get out of society and be free from all of its constraints. It is an intriguing fantasy, which Burns, like most of us, chose not to live out. Undoubtedly timidity plays some part in our avoidance. But another part is the sense that the actuality would not be so attractive as the fantasy.

In this poem Burns has daringly taken that fantasy to its conclusion. He is not concerned with its practical consequences, such as what will happen to the beggars the next day when the storm may still be raging and they've pawned their clothes for drink. Rather, he explores its psychological and ethical consequences. This is the state one reaches when one gives up the constraints of society. The beggars are admirable because they have dared to live out the potentiality of their lives to their limits. But their daring has also led to brutality.

Burns has shown the allure and the dangers not only of constraints but of freedom as well. The benevolists argued that man is intrinsically good, that if we relieve him of the constraints of society he will behave virtuously. Conservatives argued that man is intrinsically evil, that if we fail to constrain him he will behave like a beast. The conflict is one that literature, from *The Bacchae* to *An Essay on Man,* had been exploring for millennia. Usually it concluded that social limits are necessary. Burns repeatedly explored this issue in his satires and came to a somewhat different conclusion.

In "Holy Willie's Prayer" he showed the danger of excessive religious constraints. In "To a Louse" he showed the harmful effect of excessive reliance on social order. In "The Holy Fair" he argued that the natural drives will inevitably assert themselves. Now, in *Love and Liberty,* he seems to follow the adventures of the young people who leave the Holy Fair anticipating "Houghmagandie," and he takes their values and behavior to the logical and psychological conclusion.

Obviously Burns's sympathies are with the young people in the Holy Fair more than with the ranting preachers. And it is just as obvious that his sympathies are with the beggars more than with Willie or Jenny. But his sympathies for the beggars and his advocacy of their way of life are not unqualified. Unconstrained life is beautifully energetic but, taken to its limits, it can be bestial.

Love and Liberty is the greatest work of Burns's early career. It acts as a kind of summary of the themes that he has been exploring in his epistles and satires over the years 1784–85. In it he brings together his belief in freedom, his personal experiences and observations, the theories of benevolism, the techniques of Augustan satire, the models of Scottish vernacular literature, and his own brilliant common sense to create a powerful and highly persuasive argument on the strengths and the dangers of freedom. Several years later, in *Tam o'Shanter,* he will return to this theme and explore it in even greater depth.

Poems of Ordinary Life

Some of Burns's satiric poems concentrate on what is to be changed. "Holy Willie's Prayer" criticizes hypocrisy, and "To a Louse" criticizes pretentiousness. But other satiric works of Burns's contain as much affirmation as criticism. *Love and Liberty,* it could be argued, is not really a satire since it affirms the life of the beggars more than it criticizes conventional repression. Whatever we call its form, however, its subject and style are similar to another kind of Burns's poetry, descriptions of ordinary life. The difference between it and a poem like "The Cotter's Saturday Night" (K 72), written at about the same time, is not as great as at first appears. Both poems describe an aspect of ordinary life approvingly. Both denounce, less emphatically, its opposite.

Fergusson's *Farmer's Ingle* is the most important single influence on "The Cotter's Saturday Night." It contributes the idea to describe a peasant household, the use of the Spenserian stanza, and the use of allusion to other poetry. Fergusson's poem has often been praised as more realistic and less sententious than Burns's poem. But only a superficial reading of "The Cotter's Saturday Night" will uphold this judgment.

Burns enriches Fergusson's form with the ideas of contemporary English literature, especially those of Thomson, Gray, Shenstone, and possibly Goldsmith.[17] These poets describe peasant life with particular emphasis on the "goodness" of the peasants, but they do so by using a style of abstractions and generalized descriptions. Burns translates the ideas of these poets into the concrete actualities of Scottish peasant life.

"The Cotter's Saturday Night" has had one of the most varied critical careers in British literary history. Contemporary reviews singled it out as the best poem in the Kilmarnock Edition.[18] Nineteenth-century poets and critics were equally enthusiastic about it. Hazlitt described it as "a noble and pathetic picture of human manners." Byron, Scott, Francis Jeffrey, and others considered it among Burns's best works.[19] Its critical decline started in 1896, in the notes to the Henley-Henderson Centennial Edition, where the editors called it "the most artificial and most imitative of Burns's works."[20]

The low opinion of it has continued to the present, based less on Burns's imitativeness than on what is regarded as his insincerity or sentimentality. Even those who attempt to find some good in the poem show a tone of apology or condescension that is far from the adulation of most of the nineteenth century.[21] The tenth stanza in particular is suspect, with its diatribe against "A wretch! A villian! lost to love and truth! / That can . . . Betray sweet *Jenny*'s unsuspecting youth." The doubts about the sincerity of this stanza are increased when we realize that when Burns wrote it he had recently fathered one illegitimate child and had made another unmarried woman pregnant.

The critical doubts about this stanza are often applied to the remainder of the poem. Everything in the poem seems a little too pat, "The chearfu' Supper," the "artless notes," the "priest-like Father," all sound like something out of a Walt Disney film. But a friend of Burns's, Mrs. Dunlop, reports that her housekeeper, when showed the poem, "Returned the volume with a strong shaking of the head, saying, 'Nae doubt gentlemen and ladies think mickle [much] o' this, but for me its naething but what I saw i' my father's house every day, and I dinna [do not] see how he could hae tauld it ony other way.' "[22] This extraordinary tribute to Burns's accuracy and descriptive powers gives, I think, a key to the poem's value and its continuing popularity in spite of so much adverse criticism.

The poem, however, attempts more than accurate description. Burns has attempted to write a kind of sacramental poem in the eighteenth-century tradition that descends from Milton, in which a poem makes a religious statement, a poetic counterpart of a sermon. This kind of poem is not a sermon in rhyme. Rather, contemporary poets, such as Gray, Blair, Young, Smart, and Cowper, attempted to write poems that would stimulate the readers, through their response to the imagery and other poetic devices, to contemplate certain religious beliefs. In Burns's poem the religion is "New Licht" Calvinism, but it is also the religion of simplicity and of common life.

Protestantism put more emphasis on the family and on family worship than did Catholicism. In stanza 14, the father is given the role of priest, "The priest-like Father reads the sacred page." In stanza 16 the father leads in prayer, "The *Saint,* the *Father,* and the *Husband* prays." The panoply of ritual is explicitly denied in stanza 17:

> Compar'd with this, how poor Religion's pride,
>   In all the pomp of *method,* and of *art,*
> When men display to congregations wide,
>   Devotion's every grace, except the *heart*!

Most of the references are to biblical patriarchs, with the comparison to the modern, Protestant patriarch, the father of the family. The frequent references to the Bible and to *Paradise Lost* increase the sense of a ritual of ordinary life, of religion infusing the everyday. The allusions to other poetry broaden the ritual to a religion of benevolent feelings.

The simple service of stanzas 14 to 17 provides the climax to the poem. The poem starts with the day's end and the father's return, then describes a fathering of loved ones, then a simple supper, then the artless notes of singing, then the Bible reading. It starts with love in the heart, continues with the reunion of the father and his family, the love of children and parents, the love of Jenny and her *"strappan youth,"* and ends with God in the heart. Religion of the heart, then, expands to a pure love that encompasses all human relations. It is love without lust and religion without hypocrisy or pomp. At the end, the poem expands into politics, making the cotter's evening symbolic of the holiness of Scotland, "From Scenes like these, old Scotia's grandeur springs." The poem encompasses the simple religion of a peasant home, the saintly behavior of the family, the simple, heartfelt actions of meeting, supping, and singing to create a symbol that brings God into all aspects of human life and that provides an emblem of a right way to live.

Burns's theme in the poem is similar to his theme in the epistles, in "Address to the Deil," or in *Love and Liberty*: to make a sacrament out of human experience. Burns's poem evokes a religion that encompasses everything from artless peasant singing to the poetry of Pope and Milton, from conventional Christianity to a religion of the heart. Milton has told us about the holiness of the universe. Blake has told us that "Everything that lives is holy." Burns has attempted to bring Milton's holiness into ordinary experience and to show concretely how everything that lives, even the most ordinary, really is holy (something, I believe, Blake never attempted to do).

Burns created one of the few works of literature that describe life the way a poor, ordinary farmer and his family would live it and see it, related from their point of view. Modern readers tend to prefer literature that either maintains an ironic distance or that is passionately involved with its subject. In this poem Burns maintains a middle distance, telling the story from the warm but not passionate view of the cotter and his family. *They* would believe that a man who attempted to seduce Jenny would be "A wretch! a villain! lost to love and truth!" And they would see the supper as cheerful and the father as a patriarch.

It is irrelevant that we see the matters differently. This is the way the cotters see it, and apparently the way Mrs. Dunlop's housekeeper saw it.

Burns neither patronizes nor criticizes the farmer and his family. He just accepts them, the same way he accepts the rowdy behavior in "The Holy Fair" and in *Love and Liberty*. It possibly says something about us that so much contemporary criticism lauds his joyous acceptance of the beggars but holds back on his equally emotional acceptance of peasant values.

All this commentary is, admittedly, unlikely to make the poem much more enjoyable for the modern reader. But it is of some value to understand the way it was probably intended and the way it actually did appeal to just about everyone for a century. If we can, at least briefly, drop our twentieth-century jadedness perhaps we can appreciate this poem as a document of a kind of life that was once believed in.

Burns also used the ordinary life of rural Scotland symbolically in his description of the contact with animals. Animals were a popular subject in Britain in the late eighteenth century. People who believed in benevolism and the new humanitarianism began to pay attention to the rights of animals, just as they were paying greater attention to the rights of children, beggars, slaves, and other beings who had received scant attention in the past. Universalism influenced people to regard animals as creatures with feelings, both physical and emotional. Protestantism, with its greater emphasis on the life of this world, stressed the obligations of man's God-given stewardship over the lower creatures. Eighteenth-century writers—Pope, Gay, Thomson, Sterne, Smollett, Cowper, Smart, Blake, and others—often lamented cruelty to animals in hunting, in caging, and in slaughtering. But in rural Scotland, such ideas were a luxury. Life was hard, and animals, like the soil, were bound up in a frugal economy.

Burns reflected this conflict between fashionable concern and economic realities in his poetry. He wrote about animals in a variety of styles. In one of his poems, "The Twa Dogs," he adopted the old-fashioned method of giving animals human attributes, speech most notably, in order to comment on human behavior. In other poems he followed contemporary sentimental ideas. He wrote an early poem, "The Death and Dying Words of Poor Mailie," in Scottish verse form and with considerable Scottish diction, but expressing the contemporary interest in kindness to animals. In "Poor Mailie's Elegy," probably

written later, also in Scottish style, he expresses the need for kindness
and an appreciation for the usefulness of animals. In his songs, mostly
written after the Kilmarnock Edition, he often uses animals to provide
background and imagery.

But he knew animals in a kind of intimacy that was immediate, not
literary. In two poems, both written in late 1785, "To a Mouse, On
turning her up in her Nest, with the Plough, November, 1785" and
"The Auld Farmer's New-year-morning Salutation to his Auld Mare,
Maggie, on giving her the accustomed ripp of corn to hansel in the
New Year," he combines the realism of a poor Scottish farmer with the
expanding consciousness of the Enlightenment. In these poems he confronts the rarified new ideas and puts them into the context of the life
of ordinary animals.

In "To a Mouse" (K 69) Burns describes the flash of sympathy felt
by a farmer for a mouse whose nest has just been upturned by the plow.
Normally, the farmer would regard the mouse as a pest and pursue it
"Wi' murd'ring *pattle*!" But this reaction is, momentarily, different:

> Wee, sleeket, cowran, tim'rous *beastie*,   *cowering*
> O, what a panic's in thy breastie!
> Thou need na' start awa sae hasty,
>   Wi' bickering brattle!   *scurrying haste*
> I wad be laith to rin an' chase thee,   *loath; run*
>   Wi' murdering *pattle*!

In the second stanza the farmer considers the implications:

> I'm truly sorry Man's dominion
> Has broken Nature's social union,
> An' justifies that ill opinion,
>   Which makes thee startle,
> At me, thy poor, earth-born companion,
>   An' *fellow-mortal*!

"Nature's social union" is in a diction that is inconsistent with the
speech of a Scottish farmer, but the idea it expresses is appropriate.
"Nature's social union" ironically refers to those abstract schemes of the
Enlightenment that find animals and humans in benign interaction,
the ideas that were expressed in Pope's *An Essay on Man* and were
popular in Burns's time. Burns bitterly rhymes "union" with "domin-

ion," saying, as a farmer would know well, that the only "social union" is "Man's dominion."

The "startle" of the mouse, like the "cowran" and the hasty, scurrying, "bickering" movement of the second stanza, describes the physical reaction of the mouse, the movement that allows the farmer to recognize the emotion behind it. It is a response that expresses the mouse's fear and its "ill opinion" of its "earth-born companion." Through the interpretation of physical response, Burns gets into the mind of the mouse, as he gets into the minds of so many of life's outcasts. Abstract schemes, Burns says, are ludicrously irrelevant to a mouse whose house has just been destroyed. What Burns and the mouse have in common is their mortality.

In stanzas four and five Burns notes what else they have in common, typically expressed in the concrete terms of physical sensation. The "Bleak *December's winds* ensuin / Baith snell an' keen [severe and piercing]" affect the two of them, reminders of the harshness of Scottish reality. At the middle of the poem, Burns broadens its reference:

> Thou saw the fields laid bare an' wast,
> An weary *Winter* comin fast,
> An' cozie here, beneath the blast,
>   Thou thought to dwell,
> Till crash! the cruel *coulter* past
>   Out thro' thy cell.

The adjectives, "weary" and "cozie," contrast each other, and each conveys an uncomplicated, familiar physical sensation common to both beings. The "cruel *coulter*" destroys everything, leaving the mouse to "Thole [endure] the Winter's *sleety dribble,* / An' *cranreuch* [hoar frost] cauld."

The seventh stanza contains a famous quotation:

> But Mousie, thou art no thy-lane   *not alone*
> In proving *foresight* may be vain:
> The best laid schemes o' *Mice* an' *Men,*
>   Gang aft agley,   *awry*
> An' lea'e us nought but grief an' pain,
>   For promis'd joy!

Something is "agley," that is, "awry," "off the straight," "irregular," "wrong." The two companions, impoverished, cold, are united only in uncertainty. Experience justifies "ill-opinion," not "social union." Yet life offers some consolation to humans, the recognition that all living creatures share the suffering of the "weary winter" and the arbitrary threats of the "cruel coulter"; and the recognition that the fellow-feeling humans have with animals against this arbitrary, indifferent world is more important than a "*daimin-icker* in a *thrave* [an odd ear in a large measure of wheat]."

The final stanza states:

> Still, thou art blest, compar'd wi' *me*!
> The *present* only toucheth thee:
> But Och! I *backward* cast my e'e,
>   On prospects drear!
> An' *forward*, tho' I canna *see*,
>   I *guess* an' *fear*!

Burns concentrates on himself because the poem is about human consciousness, not about kindness to animals. He says that enlightened or benevolist ideas will not help the animals in the unrarified atmosphere of a poor farm. The best that these ideas can do is help human understanding, give us the strength that can come out of our feeling of fellowship with all living beings. But that is not much. The freedom described in the epistles, the pleasure described in *Love and Liberty,* and the comfort described in "The Cotter's Saturday Night" are not always available. Sometimes we are left alone, with only remembrance of "prospects drear" and fear of the future.

"The Auld Farmer's New-year-morning Salutation to his Auld Mare, Maggie, on giving her the accustomed ripp of corn to hansel in the New-Year" (K 75) is a poem that develops out of a concrete instance told with simple realism. It is in the manner of a monologue, a farmer talking to his mare on the New Year, giving her the customary gift ("to hansel") of an additional handful ("ripp") of feed. Out of this ordinary rustic incident Burns builds a poem that assesses the nature of human interaction with animals and its significance in terms of one's life.

The mare had been given to the farmer as part of his wife's dowry, twenty-nine years ago. The two have grown old together—a Scottish farmer was old in his fifties. Burns exploits all the possibilities of these ordinary facts, which allow him to discuss many of the important parts of a person's adult life: youth, love, marriage, growing old, work, and money. He doesn't need to endow the horse with human propensities, as the sentimentalists had been doing, or to endow the universe with elaborate schemes, as the Enlightenment advocated. But the poem says something important, in terms of day-to-day experience, about the relationship of humans and animals.

Burns achieves this richness of statement through a number of devices, but especially through his exploitation of the possibilities of Scottish vocabulary. In the eighteenth century Scottish words still had a particular suggestiveness, pliancy, and fullness of implication. English had undergone the rigors of the great prose writers, Addison in particular, in a way that gave greater precision but also greater restriction to its vocabulary. Scottish had no prose, and its spoken language had not been exposed to the intellectual demands of the Enlightenment (the great figures of the Scottish Enlightenment, such as David Hume and Adam Smith, wrote in English). Burns exploited this fluidity in most of his poetry, but less in his satiric than in his descriptive poems. In "The Auld Farmer's New-year-morning Salutation to his Auld Mare, Maggie," Burns exploits the possibilities of Scottish with particular effectiveness.[23]

Burns describes Maggie as a colt in terms that richly suggest the recollections of youth:

> Thou ance was i' the foremost rank,
> A *filly* buirdly, steeve an' swank,   *sturdy; firm; agile*
> An' set weel down a shapely shank,
>   As e'er tread yird;   *earth*
> An' could hae flown out-owre a stank,   *pond*
>   Like onie bird.

The adjectives of the second line are all highly suggestive, more so than their English counterparts. "Buirdly" has the sense of "burly," "stout," "strong." "Steeve" has some of the sense of "unyielding," "strong of heart." And "swank" suggests "lean," "graceful," and "attractively youthful." The adjectives all refer to the physical condition of the colt in terms appropriate for a young horse. But "steeve" and "swank" also suggest broader qualities, terms that apply to certain desirable associations with youth, such as courage and grace.

The adjectives increase in suggestiveness as the poem progresses:

> When first I gaed to woo my *Jenny,*
> Ye then was trottan wi' your Minnie:

Tho' ye was trickie, slee an' funnie,   *clever; sly; whimsical*
    Ye ne'er was donsie;   *unruly*
But hamely, tawie, quiet an' cannie,   *easy to handle; gentle*
    An' unco sonsie.   *pretty*

Burns makes the subtle association of the mare with the farmer's wife. He just mentions the courting, in a subordinate clause, but then develops the association through the adjectives, which can all be applied to a woman, especially a spirited young woman, in the way she would be recalled by her husband years later. "Sonsie" in particular is a word more commonly applied to women and has, in that context, suggestions of "buxom," "sexy," as well as "pleasant to look at." In the next stanza the farmer speaks of his wedding day, "That *day* ye pranc'd wi' muckle pride, / When ye bure hame my bonie *Bride*." And then he speaks of his pleasure in "sic a *pair*." Burns's identification of the mare and the farmer's bride conveys, simply, the emotions the farmer recalls from that happy time in his life. The beauty and high spirits of the mare combine easily with the pleasure he had in his "bonie *bride*," the way everything seems beautiful and lively when one is happy.

He recalls the sensations he had about himself and Maggie, "When thou an' I were young an' skeigh." "Skeigh" means "spirited," "proud," "mettlesome." The fun that the two of them had at fairs when they were both young and full of high spirits becomes another part of his recollections that brings the companionship between them into a common emotional experience.

Burns avoids the suggestion of sentimentality by showing the frank materialism of the farmer. The farmer recalls that the dowry that included Maggie had, equally important, "fifty mark" and adds, bluntly, "Tho it was sma', 'twas *weel-won* gear. / An' thou was stark (strong)." The changing of the generations, an aspect of growing old, is expressed in terms of the mare: "My Pleugh is now thy *bairn-time* a' [all your offsprings] / Four gallant brutes, as e'er did draw." And then, back to the frank materialism. The six other offsprings, "That thou hast nurst; / They drew me thretten pound pund an' twa." The precise figure, which he remembers over all the years, gets further emphasis through the short line, "The vera warst."

The stage that they have come to includes all the experiences they have shared. The two of them have labored together and played together, but the farmer thought alone: "An' monie an *anxious day*, I thought / We wad be beat!" Then the two rejoin, in "*crazy Age,* [broken, cracked, wobbly,] . . . Wi' something yet."

In the final stanza the first line summarizes their past, and the second describes their present together: "We've worn to crazy years thegither; / We'll toyte [totter] about wi' ane anither [one another]." In the last lines of the stanza Burns originally brought the farmer and mare closer, describing their relationship in words that were more exclusively human than any before in the poem: "An' clap [carress] thy back, / An' mind the days we've haen the gither, [had together] / An' ca' the crack [have a good chat]." Burns revised these lines to have the farmer draw slightly back from the mare, realistically separating them physically and emotionally as their lives end:

> Wi' tentie care I'll flit thy tether
>> To some hain'd rig,   *preserved ridge*
> Whare ye may nobly rax your leather,   *stretch your skin*
>> Wi' sma' fatigue.

At the end of their lives Burns does not humanize the horse and does not take the horse to heaven with the farmer. But he gives the animal's realistic counterpart of heaven to the mare.

Burns wrote in his *First Commonplace Book*: "It may be some entertainment to a curious observer of human-nature to see how a ploughman thinks, and feels, under the pressure of Love, Ambition, Anxiety, Grief with the like cares and passions, which, however diversified by the Modes, and Manners of life, operate pretty much alike I believe in all the species" (CB, 1). Burns wrote this in 1783, at the beginning of his productive period. The language of the statement is affected—"It may be some entertainment to a curious observer" and "however diversified by the Modes and Manners of life." The ideas expressed—the sentimental interest in the emotions of the noble peasant and the universalist belief in the sameness of those emotions in all "species"— might seem more appropriate for the aristocratic visitors at a London salon than for a young farmer at his plough.

Burns, however, was the first poet in British literature to express these ideas in the poetry of ordinary experience. He may have gone along with such fashionable ideas because he had not had formal education and often showed diffidence to people who appeared better educated. But he was also extraordinarily intelligent and sensitive, capable of penetrating to the heart of these ideas.

As a "curious observer of human nature" he was able to examine and describe the effects of hypocrisy and snobbery on the practitioners themselves and to work out the ramifications of total freedom. As a ploughman he was able to understand those feelings that really are basic to mankind without the encumbrances of excessive civilization. And he explored the diversification of "Modes and Manners" on "Love, Ambition, Anxiety, and Grief" in his examination of life without the constraints of classical learning, traditional literature, or arbitrary social rules.

In "The Auld Farmer's New-year-morning Salutation to his Auld Mare, Maggie," he most effectively, perhaps, of all of his poems, described the views of a ploughman that expressed universal "cares and passions." He was a poet of universal emotion described in terms of concrete, everyday experience. In this poem he was able to express, through an experience that anyone can understand, the emotions common to mankind.

In these poems written in the period from late 1784 to the end of 1785 he struggled with and expressed the integration of the popular British and European ideas and the experience he had as a poor tenant farmer; the abstractions of the Enlightenment and the racy concreteness of the Scottish literary tradition; his personal experience as a young man who was both obedient and rebellious; and the religious beliefs on two sides of a divided church. The publication of the Kilmarnock Edition, which included most of these poems, was a major stage in his life and in his career as a poet.

Chapter Three

The Songs

The Beginning of Burns's Fame

The Kilmarnock Edition was a success. A review in the *Edinburgh Magazine,* October 1786, praised Burns as a "striking example of native genius bursting through the obscurity of poverty and the obstructions of laborious life," and, although it rated Burns below Ramsay and Fergusson, it still praised the "untutored fancy" of this "common ploughman."[1] Thomas Blacklock, a blind poet of some prominence in Edinburgh, wrote to a friend about the collection, "There is a pathos and delicacy in his serious poems; a vein of wit and humour in those of a more festive turn, which cannot be too much admired, nor too warmly approved."[2] Blacklock says that Dugald Stewart, a professor of moral philosophy at the University of Edinburgh, had seen the poems; and he also says that he intends to show the poems to Hugh Blair, who was a professor of rhetoric at Edinburgh and a prominent British critic. And Blacklock expresses his hope that a second edition will be published. The first had been sold out.

Burns saw both the review and the letter. He wrote, in his autobiographical letter (R 125), "My vanity was highly gratified by the reception I met with from the Publick." He was about to depart for Jamaica, "when a letter from Dr. Blacklock to a friend of mine overthrew all my schemes by rousing my poetic ambition.—The Doctor belonged to a set of Critics for whose applause I had not even dared to hope.—His idea that I would meet with every encouragement for a second edition fired me so much that away I posted to Edinburgh without a single acquaintance in town, or a single letter of introduction in my pocket." The plans for emigration to Jamaica all but disappear. He went to Edinburgh both to investigate the possibilities of a second edition and to seek a civil service job, which he hoped would relieve him of the poverty and drudgery of farming.

Burns received an extravagant reception in Edinburgh. The city was not the important intellectual center it had been in the days of Hume and Adam Smith, but it was still a sophisticated city of considerable elegance, and the University was a center of important intellectual activity. Burns met and was befriended by both the fashionable aristocracy and the literati, in particular the critic Hugh Blair and the critic and novelist Henry Mackenzie, whose novel *The Man of Feeling* Burns had rated as one of his "bosom favorites" (R 125). Mackenzie was also editor of the *Lounger* and wrote in that periodical one of the most influential reviews of Burns's poetry.

Mackenzie's review is more enthusiastic than the review in the *Edinburgh Magazine*. He pronounces Burns a "genius [i.e., talent] of no ordinary rank." He also calls him a "Heaven-taught ploughman" and commends his " 'wood-notes wild.' "[3] The legend of Burns as the "common ploughman," the uneducated poet inspired directly from heaven, had begun.

The reception Burns received from the aristocracy in Edinburgh was consistent with the direction the critics had set. Burns fulfilled their fashionable notions, which were a vulgarized mixture of ideas in Locke, Shaftesbury, Hume, Adam Smith, Rousseau, and others, that artistic ability descends directly from heaven, uncorrupted by education or civilization. This poet-ploughman was a fulfillment of their theory.

In all fairness, Burns could be seen as having catered to this notion, as in "Epistle to J.L*****, An Old Scotch Bard":

> I am nae *Poet,* in a sense,
> But just a *Rhymer* like by chance,
> An' hae to Learning nae pretence,
>   Yet, what the matter?
> Whene'er my Muse does on me glance,
>   I jingle at her.
>
>   (ll. 49–54)

And in the preface to the Kilmarnock Edition: "Unacquainted with the necessary requisites for commencing Poet by rule, he sings the sentiments and manners he felt and saw in himself and his rustic compeers around him, in his and their native language."

The contemporary response to Burns in Edinburgh resulted from a misreading of his intent. In the Kilmarnock Edition Burns had created a particular voice, that of a simple, uneducated, farmer. It was part of the elaborate metaphor that included the apparent (but not entirely consistent) Scottish dialect, the familiar tone, the conversational rhythms, the homey images, and the everyday subjects. It was a metaphor appropriate to his theme, that creativity, like love, friendship, and pleasure, was available to everyone, a demonstration of human equality and potentiality. Burns used the style and personality of an uneducated ploughman as a means to express and represent this sentiment. The Edinburgh aristocracy and literati took him literally.

In person, Burns made no attempt to fulfill the sentimental expectations of his admirers. Contemporary reports of his behavior describe him as a graceful, witty man who affected neither lower-class manners nor amiable inferiority, a man who, in fact, occasionally displeased people with his sharp wit and his unwillingness to play the role that had been assigned to him. For example, a personal friend, Maria Riddell, describes Burns:

Devoid in great measure perhaps of those graces, of that polish, acquired only in the refinement of societies . . . though his appearance and manners were always peculiar, he never failed to delight, and to excel. . . . His features were stamped with the hardy character of independence, and the firmness of conscious, though not arrogant, pre-eminence. . . . Though nature had endowed him with a portion of the most pointed excellence in that dangerous talent [satire], he suffered it too often to be the vehicle of personal, and sometimes unfounded, animosities. . . . This however was not invariably the case; his wit . . . would lead him to the indulgence of raillery uniformly acute, but often unaccompanied with the least desire to wound.[4]

Henry Mackenzie describes him in Edinburgh: "He indulged his sarcastic humour in talking of men, particularly if he thought them proud, or disdainful of Persons of inferior rank; his Observations were always acute and forcibly expressed."[5] An early biographer reports, he "startled polite ears with the utterance of audacious epigrams, far too witty not to obtain general circulation . . . far too bitter not to produce a deep resentment."[6] When a woman in Edinburgh patronisingly invited him to dinner, without using the accepted courtesies, Burns replied that he would come if she also invited the "learned pig."[7] The aristocracy that patronized him treated him as the fulfillment of eighteenth-century sentimental claptrap. Burns did not cater to such fantasies.

His attempt to get a second edition was successful. The Edinburgh Edition of 1787 was published by William Creech, the most prominent Edinburgh publisher. The Kilmarnock Edition had been received well and had even been reviewed in London,[8] but the reception of the Edinburgh edition was much more favorable.[9] It was published in London, Belfast, Dublin, and, a few years later, in Philadelphia and New York. And the second edition began to attract the attention of other important poets. William Cowper wrote about the collection, "I think them on the whole a very extraordinary production." And Dorothy Wordsworth wrote that her brother William "had read it and admired many of the pieces very much."[10] Burns was becoming a poet who was widely known and appreciated.

He was less successful in finding a job. The rich and influential people who invited him to dinner were more interested in the idea of a ploughman poet than in helping him financially. A civil service job would have put him into the middle class, challenging their fond ideas. One person did at least find him a farm, which he worked for a period, with his usual lack of success. Eventually he did get a job in the excise as a tax collector. It was a demanding and unpleasant job whose heavy requirements took time from his writing. But it did provide him and his family with a better income and a better life than did farming.

The Choice of Songs

Another problem he faced, the most important one for us, was where to go in his writing. The Edinburgh Edition contained some new works, mostly poems that had been written earlier and excluded, for various reasons, from the Kilmarnock Edition. The poems he had written recently (e.g., "Address to Edinburgh" and "To a Haggis") are not as good as his earlier work. Possibly this decline resulted from the many pressures on him, especially his search for a new job. And he made several tours of the Scottish Highlands and Border country during this time. But his work shows an indecisiveness, a faltering. Burns makes no explicit statement that he needed a change in style, but his practice suggests that he recognized the need. He had said all he had to say through the voice of the satiric ploughman poet.

Some of the reviewers and some of his Edinburgh literary friends urged that he write in a more genteel style, with fewer Scotticisms, less bawdiness and irreligion, more in the manner of contemporary English writers such as Shenstone, Gray, and Goldsmith. Burns, for all his professed respect for these critics, did not much follow their advice in this matter. But he was influenced by their opinion in another crucial area. He began writing and collecting songs.

Burns had long shown an interest in songs. They were part of his environment in rural Scotland. In his autobiographical letter (R 125) he wrote that when he was a child, songs sung to him by an old maid of his mother's "cultivated the latent seeds of Poesy." In his teens a Collection of Songs was his "vade mecum.—I pored over them, driving my cart or walking to labor, song by song, verse by verse." He wrote songs before he wrote any other kind of poetry and had composed some forty of them by the time of the Kilmarnock Edition. But songs were also the subject of wider attention in Edinburgh and elsewhere.

Songs had been a subject of interest throughout Britain since the late seventeenth century, as is shown by the number of song collections by Ramsay, Watson, and Herd in Scotland and Bishop Percy, Hurd, and Ritson in England. The current, increasing interest was the result of the growing attention paid to simplicity in both literature and music, a reaction against the rococo elaborateness of Pope and Handel, and an expression of the new cult of the primitive.[11] In Edinburgh, song performance was the rage, and theories abounded about songs as an important art form.

The theory that exalted simplicity and that related it to the art of song was often expressed by the writers and literary theorists who befriended Burns in Edinburgh—James Beattie, Adam Ferguson, and Hugh Blair. For example, Blair writes:

Man is both a Poet and a Musician, by nature. The same impulse which prompted the enthusiastic Poetic Style, prompted a certain melody, or modulation of sound, suited to the emotions of Joy or Grief, of Admiration, Love, or Anger. . . . The Music of that early period [of the Celts and Goths] was beyond doubt extremely simple. . . . And certain it is, that from simple music only, and from music accompanied with verse or song, we are to look for strong expression, and powerful influence over the human mind. When instrumental Music came to be studied as a separate art, divested of the Poet's Song, and formed into the artificial and intricate combinations of harmony, it lost all its ancient power of inflaming the hearers with strong emotions.[12]

The songs Burns heard in Edinburgh were not as simple nor as Scottish as the songs he had heard in his village. They were, rather, a "curious blend of folk and classical music."[13] Italian ideals and Italian

singers had tampered with the folk tradition, adding fashionable flour-
ishes and emphasizing sentimentality. The interest in songs did nourish "Scotland's passionate concern for her cultural heritage, deepened
by her failure to retain political integrity."[14] But the style of songs was
slipping away from that ideal when Burns visited Edinburgh.

So for Burns, the chance to write, preserve, improve, and publish
Scottish folk songs allowed him to express many of his interests—the
development of a simple style, the union of words and music, and the
preservation and development of a form that helped to develop dis-
tinctively Scottish poetry and nourish Scottish nationalism and cultural
heritage. In particular, the simple song, devoid of "artificial and intricate combinations of harmony," gave him a form that allowed "strong
expression, and powerful influence over the human mind" and was
"suited to the emotions of Joy or Grief, of Admiration, Love, or
Anger."

In some ways, one can see the movement toward songs—or a similar
poetic form—indicated by the direction of the poems in the Kilmarnock Edition. There, the thematic and stylistic tendency is away from
a firm moral position toward one in which emotions become more
valued for themselves. In "Epistle to Davie" Burns is thankful for misfortunes because "They gie the wit of *Age* to *Youth*" (l. 91). But in "To
J.S****" he ducks "beneath Misfortune's blows" and turns to the alternative, "I rhyme away" (ll. 147,9). In "Holy Willie's Prayer" he
denounces hypocrisy. But in "Address to the Deil," he expresses
warmth to the Devil himself, "But fare you weel, auld *Nickie-ben!*"
(l. 121). In "To a Louse" he attacks Jennie's pretensions. But in *Love
and Liberty,* the Highland Widow's moral inconsistencies are just amusing, inevitable, rather lovable human failings. The interest in the poetic expression of emotions, divorced from a moral context, was the
direction Burns was headed in. Songs provided him with the appropriate form.

Burns had attempted to write a kind of poetry based on emotions
(e.g., "To Ruin," "Remorse," "Man was Made to Mourn, A Dirge,"
and "Despondency, an Ode") in a form that was distinct from the song.
In this experiment he followed some of the English poets he admired,
Gray in "Ode to Adversity," Collins in "Ode to Pity" and "Ode to
Fear," and Shenstone in "Ode to Indolence" and "Disappointment."
He was also following the moralistic, lugubrious poets of the Grave-
yard School, Blair and Young.

In "Despondency," (K 94) for example, Burns describes his mood:

> Oppress'd with grief, oppress'd with care,
> A burden more than I can bear,
>   I set me down and sigh;
> O Life! Thou art a galling load,
> Along a rough, a weary road,
>   To wretches such as I!

Burns describes a similar emotion in a song, written about a year later, "My Harry was a Gallant gay" (K 164). In this song, a woman laments "Highland Harry," who apparently was deported for his activity in the Jacobite uprising. She describes her sorrow:

> My Harry was a gallant gay,
>   Fu' stately strade he on the plain;   *strode*
> But now he's banished far awa,
>   I'll never see him back again.

> When a' the lave gae to their bed   *others*
>   I wander dowie up the glen   *lonely or dejected*
> I set me down and greet my fill,   *weep*
>   And ay I wish him back again

In both the poem and the song, Burns uses the phrase, "I set me down." In the song, the phrase follows the description of the speaker's dejected and lonely wandering. Her need to sit and weep, in isolation and sadness, contrasts with the "fu' stately" stride of her lover in the earlier stanza. And her aloneness at night in the glen becomes a touching counterpart to his banishment.

In "Despondency" the "set me down" is metaphoric. He needs to sit down and sigh because of his weariness from bearing the "galling load" of life. But the sensory additions to the metaphor convey little that we do not already know. Obviously he is weary if he has to sit down. It is equally redundant to say that he is despondent because life is galling. In the line, "oppressed with grief, oppressed with care," the nouns repeat each other and add nothing concrete to the feelings of being galled and weary. We get no help from the obvious rhymes, "care" and "bear," "load" and "road." The remainder of the poem is no better. It is riddled with fashionable vapidities and tired diction, as "How blest the Solitary's lot," with half dead metaphors, "which I too keenly taste," and with shameless imitation in the last stanza, which all but plagiarizes Gray's "Ode on a Distant Prospect of Eton College."

In "Despondency" Burns is talking about the abstract emotion. In "My Harry was a Gallant gay" he is talking about the despondency of a particular person. "Despondency" demonstrates that, however successful abstract poetry may be when written by others, Burns does not write in that style with success. "My Harry was a Gallant gay," while far from Burns's best, demonstrates how much better he can express emotion in the medium of the folk song.[15] Burns apparently recognized his limitations and began to follow the direction in which his obvious poetic powers lay, the song of emotional experience.

When we talk of Burns writing songs, we are actually referring to a complicated mixture of songwriting, song editing, and song collecting. Today we think that a person either writes original songs or preserves folk songs. But in the eighteenth century the attitude was less austere. After all, not long before Burns, established writers had been improving Shakespeare. The past was not, in the earlier eighteenth century, generally regarded as something to be preserved. By the time of Burns, the idea of historical or anthropological preservation and reconstruction was growing but was still not dominant. For most people, the past and the primitive were a kind of vast storehouse to be drawn from as one pleased. If a relic did not suit one's taste, one changed it.

The title of Allan Ramsay's collection, *Tea-Table Miscellany,* reveals that editor's intent. He collected folk songs and edited them for genteel ladies to sing in the drawing room. He carefully expurgated them of references to sex or other subjects that might offend refined taste. Other editors often purged the songs of Scotticisms, of commonplace objects, and of excessive particularity. Songs were revised to conform to the rule that literature avoid numbering the streaks of the tulip.

Burns did not usually adhere to these notions and was, by modern standards, a more reliable editor than most. As Catarina Ericson-Roos says, "Burns occupies an interesting intermediate position between these two styles" of folk song and art song. Folk songs are oral, transient, unprofessional, and have "a strong link with the past." Burns's works lean more toward the art songs, written to be printed and preserved, with professional concern for both literary and musical techniques. "Yet there are elements in many of his songs which make it impossible to conceive of them exclusively as art-songs. The themes and the style of these songs with their simplicity, their refrains, their choruses and their repetitive patterns are traditional, and a large number of the songs contain fragments of old material."[16]

Thomas Crawford has noted the various classifications into which

Burns's collected songs can be placed.[17] Burns collected and recorded some without alteration, in the manner of a modern folk-song collector. Some he altered to a "greater or lesser extent, with the idea of improving the original." In others, like "O Whistle, and I'll come to you my lad," only the chorus or a fragment remains. Others, like "A red, red Rose," are mosaics of traditional phrases. And some, like "Bessy and her spinning wheel," are entirely by Burns. Criticism of these songs, then, must take into account what was original with Burns, what was merely borrowed, and what was old but integrated with the parts that were original.

Burns's knowledge of music was extensive. A few manuscripts exist that demonstrate his ability to use musical notation. He could play the fiddle. And his correspondence with song editors demonstrates a good knowledge of musical techniques. He did not write any of the music; the airs were all traditional. When he revised a traditional song, he usually kept the words with the melody that he had heard sung with them. But at times he assigned words to other traditional tunes. When he wrote an original song he assigned it to some traditional air.

In 1787 Burns first made contact with an engraver who was compiling a collection of Scottish songs in a work called *The Scots Musical Museum.* Burns's interest was immediate. He wrote to a friend, "An Engraver, James Johnson, in Edinburgh has, not from any mercenary views but from an honest Scotch enthusiasm, set about collecting all our native Songs and setting them to music" (R 145). Burns's long-standing wish to achieve the "appelation of, a Scotch Bard" (R 90) seemed possible through the association with Johnson.

Burns became virtual editor of the collection. The first volume was about to go to press when he started work, so he had little influence on that volume. But he was editor of the next four volumes. He died before the sixth volume was started. In 1792 he began to contribute to another collection, *A Select Collection of Original Scotish Airs for the Voice,* published in London by George Thomson.

Burns wrote the words of the songs to be sung to music. He considered the interaction of words and music essential to the statement. But a discussion such as this must be limited mostly to the words. The musical annotations can be found in Kinsley's edition. A discussion of the musical techniques can be found in Catarina Ericson-Roos, *The Songs of Robert Burns: A Study of the Unity of Poetry and Music.* And excellent recordings by Ewan MacColl and Jean Redpath are available.[18] My comments will make some general references to the music.

But I strongly recommend that the reader hear some of the songs as they are sung.

The Love Songs

Burns's love songs are among his most famous. His first poem, "O once I lov'd," was written when he first fell in love, at the age of sixteen. "Thus with me began Love and Poesy" (R 125). And they continued throughout his life to be among his best works. In them he describes a range of emotions connected with love—the simple joy of being with a woman in "Green Grow the Rashes. A Fragment," the joy of love for a particular woman in "I love my Jean," protective love in "Flow Gently Sweet Afton," the sorrows of parting in "Ae Fond Kiss," the loneliness of being separated in "Mary Morrison" and "The Banks o' Doon," the joy of being married in "I hae a Wife o' my Ain."

"Green grow the Rashes. A Fragment" (K 45) is one of his most famous songs. It is early, written in August 1784 in his *First Commonplace Book*.[19] He has been speculating on such issues as the "various species of men" but decides to "wait till farther experience, & nicer observation throw more light on the subject." While waiting, he decides to "set down the following fragment which . . . is the genuine language of my heart." The decision was an extremely fortunate one, not only because it gave us this exquisite lyric, but also because it set the pattern for much of his work. The "genuine language" of his heart was to produce far better poetry than abstract speculations on "species of men."

The song is based on a popular idea—that life is full of care, but the joys of love provide a way of making it bearable. It is the carpe diem theme combined with late eighteenth-century admiration of the simple life. Phrases like "What signifies the life o' man" and "The warly [worldly] race may riches chase," with the few Scotticisms removed, could have appeared in much second-rate contemporary poetry. The strength of Burns's poem comes from his translation of this idea into such concrete experience and sensations as:

But gie me a canny hour at e'en,	*pleasant*
My arms about my Dearie, O;	
An' warly cares, an' warly men,	
May a' gae tapselteerie, O!	*topsy-turvy*

"Canny" is a rich, suggestive Scottish word that goes beyond the glossed meaning, "pleasant," or any comparable English word. It suggests "useful" and "lucky" and can describe people who are clever at business. So it suggests that the seized hour can be more shrewdly used in love than in worldly pursuits, that such an hour can bring together the sensations of feeling lucky, skillful, and pleasureful. "My arms about my Dearie, O" fixes and expresses the rich sensuousness of the experience. "Tapsalteerie" contrasts the tumultuousness of the "warly" with the stillness of lying quietly in a "canny hour at e'en."

In the following two stanzas Burns amusingly turns the Calvinist's practice of interpreting the Bible into a justification of his own morality, citing the loves of King Solomon and the creation of Eve:

> For you sae douse, ye sneer at this,   *prudent*
>   Ye're nought but senseless asses, O;
> The wisest Man the warl' saw,
>   He dearly lov'd the lasses, O.

> Auld Nature swears, the lovely Dears
>   Her noblest work she classes, O:
> Her prentice han' she tried on man,
>   An' then she made the lasses, O.

The song is mostly original but the chorus is partly based on an older song:

> Green grows the rashes—O
> Green grows the rashes—O
> The feather-bed is no sae saft
> As a bed amang the rashes.

The "bed" is then contrasted: "Yet a' the beds is na sae saft / As the bellies o' the lasses—O." Burns replaces the coarse explicitness with a suggestive analogy:

> Green grow the rashes, O;
> Green grow the rashes, O;
> The sweetest hours that e'er I spend,
>   Are spent among the lasses, O.

He does not give us the precise significance of the rashes. Instead, he allows the suggestion of freshness, naturalness, and quiet to enrich the sweet hours and to contrast the useless activity of the worldly race. The poem, then, is not a braggart's vaunting of his sexual conquests, but rather the praise of a way of life, of which sexual love is one part.

The grammatical change is notable. The original is correct Scottish. Burns drops the final "s" to make it grammatical English but ungrammatical Scottish.[20] Such changes are typical of the way Burns is indifferent to Scottish forms when they serve no poetic purpose. On the whole, his grammar is English. His vocabulary is usually English in his songs except when, as in "cannie," the Scottish word is more poetically useful.

"Green Grow the Rashes" is one of Burns's best and most famous songs, but it is not typical. Most of his love songs are written to a specific woman and have biographical relevance. The idea of Burns, popularized by early biographers, as a ruthless womanizer who used women solely for his own pleasure, who only loved "the sex," is simply not true. He was no model of chastity. But he was capable of deep love for women, and his relationships were those of genuine attachments. He did brag about his prowess a few times. His actions, however, were humane, responsible, and loving. In 1788 his relationships with two women, and his deep love for one of them, influenced the style of his love songs so that the songs became much more specific, directed to individual women.

Burns met Jean Armour, a young woman from his village, in 1785, when he was writing the poems that would appear in the Kilmarnock Edition. She became pregnant with his child in early 1786, and Burns gave her some paper that acknowledged her as his wife. Although he had had affairs with other women before and possibly during the time of his affair with Jean, Jean was the one he loved and wanted to marry. But her parents repudiated the marriage because Burns was from a slightly lower social class than they were and because he had a questionable reputation. Jean acceded to her parents' demand. Her father, with questionable legality, destroyed the acknowledgment of marriage that Burns had given to Jean.

Burns was deeply angered by the Armours' snobbery and Jean's betrayal. He unquestionably loved her, as his letters and poems frequently attest, and he regarded her rejection as one more instance of his cursed luck. But he had no power to change the decision. The two of them stood on the "cutty-stool" in church for three Sundays to hear the minister denounce them for the sin of fornication, and they were pronounced bachelor and spinster. In September she bore him twins.

After the success of the Kilmarnock Edition, Jean's family had a change of heart and agreed to the marriage. Burns triumphantly refused.

Burns met Agnes Craig M'Lehose in Edinburgh in late 1787. She was a married woman, separated from her husband and steeped in the sentimental extravagances of contemporary fashion. The two were soon in the throes of a passionately sentimental but chaste affair, reflected in their gushy pen names for each other, "Sylvander" and "Clarinda." Burns wrote, in a typical letter: "O Clarinda! shall we not meet in a state, some yet unknown state of Being, where the lavish hand of Plenty shall minister to the highest wish of Benevolence; and where the chill north-wind of Prudence shall never blow over the flowery fields of Enjoyment?" (R 166).

Burns continued to see Jean Armour during the time that he was seeing Clarinda. He wrote to a friend about Jean only a few weeks after the above quoted letter to Clarinda: "Jean I found banished, like a martyr—forlorn destitute and friendless . . . I have taken her a room. I have taken her to my arms . . . And I have f———d her till she rejoiced with joy unspeakable. . . . I swore her privately and solemnly never to attempt any claim on me as a husband" (R 215).[21]

And at the same time he wrote to Clarinda about Jean: "I am disgusted with her; I cannot endure her! I, while my heart smote me for the prophanity, tried to compare her with my Clarinda. . . . Here was tasteless insipidity, vulgarity of soul, and mercenary fawning; there, polished good sense, heaven-born genius, and the most generous, the most delicate, the most tender Passion" (R 210).

Burns's treatment of both women was horrendous. But his good feelings for Jean were, finally, the genuine ones. In spite of the coarseness of his description, he expresses true concern for Jean's condition. And his talk of the generous, delicate, tender passion for Clarinda has the hollow ring (as does most of his correspondence with her) of someone playing a part. It is hardly surprising, then, that in April, 1788 he returned to Ayrshire and acknowledged Jean as his wife. He describes his decision: "This was not in consequence of the attachment of romance perhaps; but I had a long and much-loved fellow creature's happiness or misery in my determination, and I durst not trifle with so important a deposit. Nor have I any cause to repent it. If I have not got polite tattle, modish manners, and fashionable dress, I am not sickened and disgusted with the multiform curse of boarding-school affectation; and I have got the handsomest figure, the sweetest temper, the soundest constitution, and the kindest heart in the country" (R 272).

So Clarinda's "polished good sense" has changed to "boarding-school affectation," and Jean's "tasteless insipidity" and "vulgarity of soul" have changed to "sweetest temper" and "kindest heart." Perhaps pity and a sense of responsibility played some part in his decision. But love played a larger part. He says that he loves her "near to distraction" (R 254).

Burns's choice seems right. All reports describe Jean as a decent, generous, unpretentious woman with a simple, appropriate dignity. She adopted one of his illegitimate children, bore him five more (in addition to the children born before their marriage), and put up with his occasional wanderings. He remained married, although not entirely faithful to her, and she remained a loving and understanding wife. We hear few words of complaint from Burns about her.

The choice between Jean Armour and Agnes M'Lehose is reflected in his choice of style of poetry. He wrote two songs, "Clarinda" and "I love my Jean," within a few months of each other. He wrote about Agnes M'Lehose:

> Clarinda, mistress of my soul,
>   The measur'd time is run!
> The wretch beneath the dreary pole,
>   So marks his latest sun.
> . . . .
> She, the fair Sun of all her sex,
>   Has blest my glorious day:
> And shall a glimmering Planet fix
>   My worship to its ray?
>   ("Clarinda," K 217)

And he wrote about Jean, in an original song composed for her during their honeymoon:

> I see her in the dewy flowers,
>   I see her sweet and fair;
> I hear her in the tunefu' birds,
>   I hear her charm the air:
> There's not a bony flower, that springs
>   By fountain, shaw, or green;   *thicket*

> There's not a bony bird that sings
> But minds me o' my Jean.
> ("I love my Jean," K 227)

The language of "Clarinda" is a pastiche of borrowed phrases from such disparate sources as MacKenzie's *Man of Feeling* and Young's *Night Thoughts*. The problem, however, is not that Burns borrowed the phrases (his songs are full of borrowings) but that he fails to turn them into concrete expression. We learn little about Burns's feelings when he tells us that his "glorious day" is blest by a "fair sun." The song is an attempt to write love poetry in the style of "Despondency," and with no more success.

In "I love my Jean," the effect of the poem comes from Burns's just touching on the sensations, but touching on many of them—sight, touch, sound. And these sensations are detailed in several ways—color, movement, the sense of water from the fountain and the dew, shape from the flower and the thicket. So the poem works through the use of many brief sensations rather than the deeper exploration of a single sensation. It is in the lighter, more suggestive style of "Green Grow the Rashes," "But gie me a canny hour at e'en, / My arms about my Dearie, O."

This style is typical of many of Burns's best songs—the use of physical sensations just touched on, simple diction, and the avoidance of complex conceits and extended images. These techniques all contribute to the special form of a song, which is meant to be heard. The listener must experience the sensation easily and briefly; he needs simple language, cannot follow elaborate metaphors, and cannot consult a glossary to understand the Scottish words.

The simple style is also appropriate for the kind of statement Burns has chosen to make, a statement that relies on the primacy of universally available emotions. The emotion evoked by the sensations of a dewy flower and a tuneful bird is more generally accessible than the emotion that comes from deciphering baroque images of the sun at the pole. When Burns chose Jean Armour over Agnes M'Lehose, he chose a "clean-limb'd, handsome bewitching young Hussy" (R 237) over a woman of "polished good sense, heaven-born genius, and . . . the most tender Passion." He also chose a "farthing taper" over "the cloudless glory of the meridian sun" (R 210). Obviously the farthing taper made for a better style of poetry.

He held to this style in his best love poems, using the sensations of

color, shape, sound, sleeping and waking, smell, taste, touch, coolness
and warmth, to convey a range of emotions. For example the use of
gentle sound to express quiet love:

> Hark, the mavis' evening sang   *thrush*
> Sounding Clouden's woods amang;
> Then a faulding let us gang,   *sheep gathering; go*
>   My bonie Dearie.
> ("Ca' the Yowes to the knowes," K 456)

Or sound and color to express protective love:

> Thou stock dove whose echo resounds thro' the glen,
> Ye wild whistling blackbirds in yon thorny den,
> Thou green crested lapwing thy screaming forbear,
> I charge you disturb not my slumbering Fair.
>   ("Afton Water," K 257)

Or taste and sound to express love turned to hate:

> Wha I wish were maggots' meat,   *who*
> Dish'd up in her winding sheet;
> I could write—but Meg maun see 't—   *might*
>   Whistle o'er the lave o't.
> ("Whistle o'er the lave o't," K 235)

And coolness and sound to express the death of love:

> Blest be the hour she cool'd in her linnens,
> And blythe be the bird that sings on her grave!"
>   ("Merrie hae I been," K 305).

The Merry Muses of Caledonia

Burns also wrote poems about sex, in his collection called *The Merry
Muses of Caledonia*. The collection was not intended for publication,
was not published during his lifetime, and has had a troubled publishing history. Through the years, innumerable bawdy poems were attributed to Burns. Only recently has there been a scholarly attempt to
identify the genuine ones.[22]

The songs are often witty and lively. In them he covers some of the same subjects as in other songs, such as the theme that sex is one of the few pleasures allowed to the poor:

> When Princes and Prelates & het-headed zealots
>   All Europe has set in a lowe,   *flame*
> The poor man lies down, nor envies a crown,
>   And comforts himsel with a mowe.
>   ("When Princes and Prelates," K 395)

He satirizes the Calvinist doctrine of salvation through faith by having a priest say to a troubled woman:

> What signifies Morals and Works,
>   Our works are no wordy a runt!   *worthy*
> It's Faith that is sound orthodox,
>   That covers the fauts o' your————.
>   (I'll tell you a tale of a Wife," K 277)

And he speaks of the joys of sex while satirizing classical forms:

> There Damon lay, with Sylvia gay,
>   To love they thought no crime, Sir;
> The wild-birds sang, the echoes rang,
>   While Damons's a————se beat time, Sir
>   ("Ode to Spring-," K 481)

On the whole, the poems of *The Merry Muses of Caledonia* are disappointing. The songs tend to be satiric and clever, written in a style more reminiscent of Restoration poetry than in the sensuous manner of Burns's contemporaries (e.g., John Cleland in *Memoirs of a Woman of Pleasure*). Considering that Burns wrote so much about sex, was relatively free from the repression and distortion that have haunted much of poetry, and was so skilled at conveying physical sensation, we might have expected some outstandingly successful examples of poetic pornography.

One song in this collection that uses sensuousness satirically is "The Fornicator. A New Song" (K 61). It may describe Burns's appearance with Elizabeth Paton, a servant of his mother's, before the church court for the sin of fornication:

Before the Congregation wide
  I pass'd the muster fairly,
My handsome Betsey by my side,
  We gat our ditty rarely;   *received our reproof*
But my downcast eye by chance did spy
  What made my lips to water,
Those limbs so clean where I, between,
  Commenc'd a Fornicator.

Burns juxtaposes his erring sexual thoughts and watering lips with the church's reprimand, satirically reminding us of the inevitability of physical drives and the ineffectuality of moral tyranny.

Burns treated the same subject a few months later, in a song written for *The Scots Musical Museum*. It is spoken by an unmarried woman who knows she is pregnant and thinks of the consequences with practicality and optimism:

O Wha my babie-clouts will buy,   *baby clothes*
O Wha will tent me when I cry;   *take care of me*
Wha will kiss me where I lie,
The rantin dog the daddie o't.
("The rantin dog the Daddie o't," K 80)

She foresees the church punishment to be meted out to herself and her lover: the two of them forced to stand on the cutty-stool before the congregation:

When I mount the Creepie-chair,
Wha will sit beside me there,
Gie me Rob, I'll seek nae mair,
The rantin dog the Daddie o't.

What will crack to me my lane;   *talk to me alone*
Wha will mak me fidgin fain;   *physically excited*
Wha will kiss me o'er again,
The rantin dog the Daddie o't.

The description stops just short of intercourse—the physical excitement, the kissing—substituting a sense of high spirits and physical pleasure. The speaker in "The Fornicator," through his bragging tone—"But a bonny lass upon the grass . . . O that's a fornicator"—

draws attention to himself. The joyous tone of "The rantin dog" makes the point that the best revenge against moral tyranny is personal pleasure. The words of "The rantin dog" are set to a spirited air that emphasizes every second syllable (e.g., "Wha," "crack," "me," "lane"), repeats the melody for each line, and lands strongly on the rhyme word. The music effectively supports the sense of high spirits, optimism, and indifference to religious condemnation. It is in his suggestive rather than in his explicitly sexual poems that Burns is most successful.

Many of his poems are actually tidied up versions of older bawdy songs, usually improving the original. I noted earlier his improvements in "Green Grow the Rashes, O." "Duncan Gray" (earlier version, K 204) is another such improvement. One part of the original runs:

He kiss'd her butt, he kiss'd her ben,	*outside; inside*
He bang'd a thing against her wame;	
But, troth, I now forget its name;	
But, I trow, she gat the girdin' o't.	*swear; riding*

Burns changes this to:

The girdin brak, the beast cam down,	*strap broke*
I tint my curch and baith my shoon,	*lost; kerchief; both shoes*
And Duncan ye're an unco loon;	*big lout*
Wae on the bad girdin o't,	*damn*

Burns loses the witty pun on "butt" and "ben." But he makes the song more subtly effective. The change from "bang'd a thing" to "The beast cam down," the shift from details of intercourse to the result of it, the elimination of the awkwardly coy "I now forget its name" keep most of the humor of the original and reduce the coarseness. The change of speaker from observer to participant, her amusing details of the loss of her kerchief and "baith" her shoes, her straightforward, racy cursing of Duncan add psychological and human dimensions.

This tendency, to try to improve songs by removing indecencies, was not always successful. "John Anderson my Jo" (K 302) for example:

> John Anderson my jo, John,
>   When we were first acquent;
> Your locks were like the raven,
>   Your bony brow was brent;   *smooth*
> But now your brow is beld, John,   *bald*
>   Your locks are like the snaw;
> But blessings on your frosty pow,   *head*
>   John Anderson my Jo.

It is based on a bawdy song, which now sounds like a parody on Burns's rather sentimental song.

> John Anderson, my jo, John,
>   When first that ye began,
> Ye had as good a tail-tree
>   As ony ither man;
> But now its waxen wan, John,
>   And wrinkles to and fro;   *wriggles*
> I've two gae-ups for ae gae down,
>   John Anderson, my jo.

Perhaps Burns could be a prude at times. But sensuous description of sexuality presents problems. The older, witty pornography—Rochester's, for example—mostly just makes us laugh. Sensuous pornography has a way of rousing sexual feelings so powerfully that everything else is excluded. Burns is most effective when he uses sensory imagery to convey emotions. "I see her in the dewy flowers" conveys sweet love, and "Wha I wish were maggots' meat" conveys hate. But sensuous sexual writing usually conveys only sexual titilation. And Burns was a poet of the emotions.

Social and Ethical Songs

In other songs Burns deals with broader issues. But he concentrates on the emotion that is related to the issue. In the late poems of the Kilmarnock period he focused on the conflict felt rather than on the issues that might resolve the conflict. "Address to the Deil," for example, described the variance between rationalism and belief in the Devil rather than the philosophical arguments for one side or the other. In many of the songs Burns takes this approach further, focusing entirely on the feeling. For example, an important ethical issue in Burns's time was whether parents had the right to decide whom their offspring should marry. In "Tam Glen" (K 236) Burns portrays the lament of a young woman who is in love with a young man whom her parents disapprove of. Burns takes no moral position. He simply focuses on the human predicament—what it feels like to be divided between love and filial duty:

> My heart is a breaking, dear Tittie,   *sister*
>   Some counsel unto me come len';
> To anger them a' is a pity,
>   But what will I do wi' Tam Glen?

Burns does not say that the parents are tyrannical or that the girl is disobedient. He just respects the emotion, which he conveys through ordinary detail, through the persistent repetition of Tam's name, and through comparisons that touchingly express both the irrationality and the power of young love:

> There's Lowrie the laird o' Dumeller,
>   'Gude day to you brute' he comes ben: *inside*
> He brags and he blaws o' his siller,   *silver*
>   But when will he dance like Tam Glen.

As Kinsley notes, she "is a complex of tenderness and prudence, dismay and assurance, anxiety and sly humour. . . . and there are touches of irony in her appeal to her sister":

> Come counsel, dear Titty, don't tarry;
>   I'll gie you my bonny black hen,
> Gif ye will advise me to Marry   *if*
>   The lad I lo'e dearly, Tam Glen.

Burns set the words to an old air, a simple melody with a repetitive, almost monotonous beat. "The rather flat melody . . . nicely sustains the girl's persistent chatter and her proccupation with the reiterated 'Tam Glen.' "[23] There is little pause at the end of each line, so the rhythm gives the sense of a breathless, almost obsessive speaker. And the double beat at the end of each stanza, where there is a distinct pause, further emphasizes the attraction of the sound of his name.

Burns treats this theme, with a variation, in a later song, "O Whistle, and I'll come to you my lad" (K 420). The chorus is mostly traditional:

> O whistle, and I'll come to you my lad,
> O whistle, and I'll come to you my lad,
> Tho father and mother and a' should go mad,
>   Thy Jeanie will venture wi' ye my lad.

The last line of the chorus is Burns's, lending it a touching reference to his love for Jean Armour and her parents' objection to the marriage. The body of the song, probably original, is a dramatic monologue that develops the young woman's character and explores her feelings:

> At kirk, or at market whene'er ye meet me,
> Gang by me as tho' that ye car'd nae a flie;
> But steal me a blink o' your bonie black e'e,
>   Yet look as ye were na lookin at me—
>   Yet look as ye were na lookin at me.

She is more assertive than the speaker in "Tam Glen." She is ready to offend her parents and she directs her lover's behavior. But her assertiveness is softened by her admiration for his "bonie black e'e" and her need for his momentary reassurance.

The music has three beats to the line, with the third beat the strongest. In this stanza the strong beat lands on "car'd" and the first syllable of "bonie," thus highlighting the need of the speaker to be unsuspected and reassured at once. And again, Burns captures the excitement of an emotion, fixing it in a situation in which consequences and obligations are irrelevant. The feeling has its own reality.

Burns wrote a song expressing the dangers of impulsive, imprudent, disobedient marriage in "Jumpin John" (K 199):

Her Daddie forbad, her Minnie forbad;	
Forbidden she wadna be:	*would not*
She wadna trow't, the browst she brew'd	*believe; brew she made*
Wad taste sae bitterlie.	

"Jumpin John" is mostly a patchwork of older songs. "Tam Glen" and "O, Whistle, and I'll come to you my Lad" are largely original with Burns. This is fairly typical of Burns, to state conventional ideas in revised older songs and to explore current ideas in original ones.

In these songs he is exploring the issue of a child's responsibility to parents, but his treatment is the same for all social and ethical issues. He usually offers no resolution. The traditional solution would be for the girl to obey her parents. The enlightened approach would portray the parents as tyrannical. The reality is always more complex, as Burns knew well. He dealt with the conflict by going to the feeling of the problem, not to a simplistic solution on one side or the other. He extolled the emotion itself—of sexual love, youthful impulsiveness, filial duty, and the pain of divided loyalty.

Political Songs

Burns addressed political issues similarly to the way he addressed social and ethical issues, particularly in his treatment of Jacobite songs. The Scottish Jacobite folk songs described incidents surrounding the Scottish Highland's support of Charles Stuart, "Bonnie Prince Charlie," the pretender to the British throne. The support is hard to understand. Prince Charles would have brought little freedom or independence to Scotland. His Catholicism would have been anathema. But he had a Scottish surname, and he was opposed to the government in London. That was enough for many Scots. For one glorious year Prince Charles had held court in Edinburgh, and Scottish Highland troops, with tartans and bagpipes, had fought the English openly. The memory of the Battle of Culloden was still fresh and a rich source for symbolism of the mystique of Scotland.

Burns's views on the politics of the issues were more sensible than those of most Scotsmen. He shared their attraction to Prince Charles as a symbol of Scottish nationhood, but he also recognized that life was probably better under the Hanovers. It was another unresolvable problem, between his love for the Scottish mystique and his commonsensical support of a united Britain. As usual, he avoided an arbitrary resolution. Instead, he wrote about the war's emotional effect.

"My Harry was a Gallant gay," discussed earlier, is one example. Another is "It was a' for our rightfu' king" (K 589). The original folk song on which Burns based this song relates the trooper's heroic farewell to his love. Burns limits the farewell to the first three stanzas, then gives the last two, which are original, to the sorrow of the woman waiting. The last stanza reads:

When day is gane, and night is come,
  And a' folk bound to sleep;
I think on him that's far awa,
  The lee-lang night and weep, my dear,   *live long*
  The lee-lang night and weep.

The poem is neither militarist nor pacifist, for feeling is what matters here, not the political conflict. Even in "My bony Mary" (K 242) where Burns evokes the excitement and pageantry of war and creates "the whole atmosphere of medieval romance and martial ballad,"[24] he still returns to the simple human feeling. In a stanza entirely original, a man is the speaker:

The trumpets sound, the banners fly,
  The glittering spears are ranked ready,
The shouts o' war are heard afar,
  The battle closes deep and bloody.
It's not the roar o' sea or shore,
  Wad make me langer wish to tarry;
Nor shouts o' war that's heard afar—
It's leaving thee, my bony Mary!

Songs of Pleasure

Between late 1789 and the end of 1792, Burns wrote a number of songs that celebrate the pleasures of life. Just why these contented works come at this time is a bit difficult to explain. In his letters he reports that his depression has continued. "My nerves are in a damnable State.—I feel that horrid hypochondria pervading every atom of both body & soul" (R 381). His health was bad, from a number of causes, but particularly from symptoms of the cardiac infection that would soon kill him. He was troubled with support of an illegitimate child from his past, and he had at least one more affair, which produced yet another child.

On the other hand, he started his job in the excise at about this time. His feelings about the job were mixed, but it relieved him of the constant financial and physical burden that farming had entailed. His songwriting and collecting were obviously going well, and his fame was growing. He wrote his greatest poem during this period, *Tam o'Shanter*.

And the political scene was at one of those rare moments in history when things did really seem to be hopeful. The American Revolution, which Burns (like many other British) sympathized with, had succeeded. The French Revolution was exhilarating in its early years to many British liberals. The Reign of Terror had not yet begun. The politics in Britain was showing signs of new vigor, a democratic political movement was underway, and there was hope for badly needed reform. The Anti-Sedition laws had not yet been passed.

Burns does not much discuss politics in his poetry of these years. But some of the themes that run through this period are cognate with the political causes he sympathized with: joy in personal independence and joy in manual labor. And his happy personal life is reflected in his poems about joy in marriage. In one song he adapts an old song to combine the themes of personal independence with happy marriage:

> I hae a wife o' my ain, *own*
> I'll partake wi' naebody;
> I'll tak Cuckold frae nane,
> I'll gie Cuckold to naebody.
> ("I hae a wife o' my ain," K 361)

In another song Burns expresses the exuberant joy of work and married love, in "Merry hae I been teethin a heckle" (K 305):

> O Merry hae I been teethin a heckle, *flax comb*
> An' merry hae I been shapin a spoon:
> O merry hae I been cloutin a kettle,
> A' kissin my Katie when a' was done.
> O, a' the lang day I ca' at my hammer, *drive*
> An' a' the lang day I whistle and sing;
> O, a' the lang night I cuddle my kimmer, *wife*
> An' a' the lang night as happy's a king.

In "Bessy and her spinning wheel" (K 365) he evokes the quiet contentment of a woman who is satisfied to sit spinning and enjoying her pastoral surroundings. The song combines the joy of work with the pleasures of nature and independence:

> O leeze me on my spinnin-wheel, *I love*
> And leeze me on my rock and reel;
> Frae tap to tae that cleeds me bien, *from head to toe; clothes me warmly*
> And haps me fiel and warm at e'en! *wraps me cosily*

I'll set me down and sing and spin,
While laigh descends the simmer sun   *low*
Blest wi' content, and milk and meal,
O leeze me on my spinnin-wheel.
. . . .
On lofty aiks the cushats wail,   *oaks; wood-pigeon*
And Echo cons the doolfu' tale;
The lintwhites in the hazel braes,   *linnets; slopes*
Delighted, rival ithers lays: *each other's*
The craik amang the claver hay,   *corncraik; clover*
The paitrick whirrin o'er the ley,   *partridge; lea*
The swallow jinkin round my shiel,   *darting; hut*
Amuse me at my spinnin wheel.

Wi' sma' to sell, and less to buy,
Aboon distress, below envy,   *above*
O wha wad leave this humble state,
For a' the pride of a' the Great?
Amid their flairing, idle toys,
Amid their cumbrous, dinsome joys,   *noisy*
Can they the peace and pleasure feel
Of Bessy at her spinnin wheel!

Though the sentiment is commonplace for the period, note how Burns
conveys it through the speaker's sensations—the warm clothing, the
balance of "sing" with "spin" and of "content" with "milk and meal."
In the last stanza Burns changed "empty joys" to the more sensuous
"dinsome joys," which contrasts the "din" of the city with the uncomplicated emotions conveyed by the sounds of nature—the wailing of
the wood-pigeons and the delighted rivalry of the linnets. The "jinkin"
of the swallows conveys not only rapid movement but high spirits,
which contrasts the "cumbrous" joys of the city. It is surely one of the
most successful portrayals of rustic contentment in the language.

And he expresses the pleasures of drinking and getting drunk with
old friends. Perhaps his most successful drinking song is "Willie
brew'd a peck o' maut" (K 268), written about a specific meeting with
two friends:

O Willie brew'd a peck o' maut,   *malt*
    And Rob and Allen cam to see;

> Three blyther hearts, that lee lang night,
>   Ye wad na found in Christendie.

Burns brilliantly exploits the chorus:

> We are na fou, we're nae that fou,   *drunk*
>   But just a drappie in our e'e;
> The cock may craw, the day may daw,   *crow; dawn*
>   And ay we'll taste the barley bree.   *brew*

In each stanza they get drunker, so the repeating choral insistence that "We are na fou, we're nae that fou" accurately describes a drunken party:

> It is the moon, I ken her horn,
>   That's blinkin in the lift sae hie;   *sky so high*
> She shines sae bright to wyle us hame,   *lure*
>   But by my sooth she'll wait a wee!
>   Cho. We are nae fou &c.

> Wha first shall rise to gang awa,
>   A cuckold, coward loun is he!   *lout*
> Wha first beside his chair shall fa',
>   He is the king amang us three!
>   Cho. We are nae fou &c.

Ericson-Roos points out that the melody is full of "skips and leaps, ascents and descents . . . but it is particularly the unpredictability of the rhythm . . . which capture[s] the drunken abandon perfectly."[23] And Daiches observes that the song is "wholly lacking in the self-conscious swaggering note found in so many English drinking songs of the century; it is a frank celebration of drunkenness, derived from a specific social occasion and anchored solidly in experience. . . . Few poets have had Burns's skill at distilling a mood of total abandonment to the pleasures of the moment."[26]

It is pleasant to speculate that during these years Burns achieved contentment, peace, and hope. He had had pleasure and excitement in his life before, but he was often disturbed by depressions or serious external problems. Now, for the first time, he had financial security and the feeling of independence that often goes with it. His health was

not good, but he expected it to get better. He enjoyed his wife and
children, his work, his recognition, and a political scene that held
considerable promise for the causes that he believed in.

Imagery in the Songs

In the songs Burns used physical images to convey and express emotions. The images concentrate on a brief sight or sensation, an action
briefly described, a fragmentary thought or wish, a recollection, a
quick comparison, such as, "I see her in the dewy flowers," "Wha I
wish were maggot's meat," "Wha will mak me fidgin fain," "But steal
me a blink o' your bonie black e'e," and "Merry hae I been shapin' a
spoon." They do not draw attention to the sensation itself but rather
direct the reader's response to the emotion the sensation is intended to
evoke. Compare, for example, the way Burns describes joyous love and
abandoned love:

> O my Luve's like a red, red rose,
>   That's newly sprung in June:
> O my Luve's like the melodie
>   That's sweetly play'd in tune.
>   ("A red red Rose," K 453)

> Simmer's a pleasant time,
>   Flowers of every colour;
> The water rins o'er the heugh,   *bank*
>   And I long for my true lover.
>   ("Ay waukin O," K 287)

In the first poem Burns gives us two distinct sensations. Both are force-
fully but briefly described. The combination of a bright color and a
sweet melody, the concreteness of the single rose, and the proper tonal-
ity of the melody create the vividness, excitement, and sweetness of a
strong, happy love.[27] In the second song the images are elusive. The
speaker seems barely aware of what colors the flowers are. It is not clear
which of her senses the water plays on—does she see it, hear it, or just
vaguely recall it? The blurred images convey the numbness of lost love.
The sensuous images in both poems direct us to the emotion of the
speaker.

Burns fulfilled Blair's prescription for creating a poetry of "strong expression, and powerful influence over the human mind." He found the devices of language, imagery, and music that would create this effect with simplicity and directness. He fit the words to "a certain melody, or modulation of sound, suited to the emotions of Joy or grief, of Admiration, Love, or Anger." Blair had sentimentally speculated on the existence of such ancient songs, which had the "power of inflaming the hearer with strong emotions." Burns actually created them.

And Burns went further. By having the emotions arise from a social or political context, but then allowing them to have their own justification, he enacted his belief in the value of human emotions. They become more important than the traditional or ideological schemes in which they occur. In celebrating these emotions over schemes that had always been regarded as more important (e.g., filial duty, political loyalty, the obligations of work), he may have created in these songs a greater respect for human feelings as such than poetry had ever seen before.

Revolutionary Songs

Curiously, a few of Burns's most famous songs are not typical of his style. The best of them are written late in his life and express the exhilaration of the early years of the French Revolution.

"Scots Wha Hae" (K 425) is ostensibly a Scottish patriotic song. Burns reports, however, that it was as much a song about the French Revolution (it was written in 1793) as about the ancient Scottish war for independence under Wallace: "I had no idea of giving myself any trouble on the Subject, till the accidental recollection of the glorious struggle for Freedom, associated with the glowing ideas of some other struggles of the same nature, *not quite so ancient,* roused my rhyming Mania" (R 582). The song is a call both to Scottish nationalism and to the democratic spirit of the nineties inspired by the French Revolution:

> Wha for Scotland's king and law,   *who*
> Freedom's sword will strongly draw,
> Free-man stand, or Free-man fa',
>   Let him follow me.
> . . . .
> Lay the proud Usurpers low!
> Tyrants fall in every foe!

> Liberty's in every blow!
> Let us Do—or Die!!!

Some may agree with Daiches, that it is "essentially a rhetorical poem of slogans and exhortations. . . . an English sentimental poem on liberty in the eighteenth-century sense."[28] Yet it has been extraordinarily popular, especially in Scotland.

"Is there for honest Poverty" (K 482), one of the important songs of democratic revolution, is told mostly in abstractions. The ideas of the poem, as Kinsley points out,[29] are generally conventional, some going back to Restoration drama—the contempt for the prancing aristocrat, the praise for the simple, decent man. Some were expressed by Pope in *An Essay on Man* (4.167–257) (e.g., "Honour and shame from no Condition rise" [1.193]). But many of the ideas are similar to those of Thomas Paine in his *The Rights of Man*. Although there is no evidence that Burns read Paine, Paine's ideas were popular and could have come to Burns through any number of sources in the early 1790s. The ideas may have been old, but the poem gets its force from the democratic fervor of its time, which Paine had expressed eloquently. Its power comes from directness, firmness of statement, and sureness of conviction, especially in the last stanza:

> Then let us pray that come it may,
>   As come it will for a' that,
> That Sense and Worth, o'er a' the earth
>   Shall bear the gree, and a' that.   *come off best*
> For a' that, and a' that,
>   Its comin yet for a' that,
> That Man to Man the warld o'er.
>   Shall brothers be for a' that.

"Scots Wha Hae" and "Is there for honest Poverty" attest to Burns's ability to reach many people. Both songs express the democratic fervor of the period and the demand for personal and political freedom from oppression that has remained a legacy of Europe and America since the late eighteenth century. Burns could touch the heart in a great many ways.

The Last Years

After 1792 life became harder for Burns. His health declined. The demands of his job increased, and the income decreased. He worried about dying and leaving his family without financial support. In a letter to his friend, Frances Dunlop, he expresses his concern and his love for his family: "There had much need be many pleasures annexed to the states of husband & father, for God knows, they have many peculiar cares.—I cannot describe to you, the anxious, sleepless hours these ties frequently give me. I see a train of helpless little folks. . . . If I am nipt off at the command of Fate . . . what would become of my little flock!—'Tis here that I envy your people of fortune.—A Father on his deathbed, taking an everlasting leave of his children, is indeed woe enough; but the man of competent fortune leaves his sons & daughters independency & friends; while I—but my God, I shall run distracted if I think any longer on the Subject!—" (R 605). He quotes an old Scots ballad:

O that I had ne'er been married,
 I would never had nae care;
Now I've gotten wife and bairns,   *children*
 They cry, Crowdie! evermair.   *meal*

Later he added an original stanza to the song, in his distinctive, sensuous, concrete style:

Waefu' Want and Hunger fley me,   *woeful; terrify*
 Glowrin' by the hallan en';   *glowering; house end*
Sair I fecht them at the door,   *sorely; fought*
 But ay I'm eerie they come ben. *apprehensive; into the inner room*
  ("O that I had ne'er been Married,"
      K 604)

He continued to believe in the French Revolution, but he saw the British support for that movement waning. British politics was turning toward greater oppression, and the fledgling British democratic movement was in trouble. Psychological depressions continued to plague him, aggravated by his bad health and family worries. In February 1794, he wrote: "For these two months I have not been able to lift a pen. My constitution and frame were, *ab origine,* blasted with a deep incurable taint of hypochondria, which poisons my existence. Of late a number of domestic vexations, and some pecuniary share in the ruin of these ***** times . . . have so irritated me, that my feelings at times could only be envied by a reprobate spirit listening to the sentence that dooms it to perdition" (R 619).

In late 1792 he started working with George Thomson, editor of *A Select Collection of Scottish Airs for the Voice* published in London. The association was bad. James Johnson, the editor of *The Scots Musical Museum,* had been grateful for Burns's help and had allowed him a free hand. But Thomson had no sense of Burns's genius and apparently thought of him as little better than a hack who would produce the purified, genteel songs that were conventional in eighteenth-century collections. He lectured Burns on poetry and music, arrogantly insisting on changes that were almost always for the worse. For example, he objected to "Comin thro' the rye" because young ladies might not like to sing about kissing.[30] Under Thomson's influence, Burns returned, reluctantly, to writing songs in the tired neoclassical idiom of "Clarinda," the style that he had pretty much abandoned since his marriage to Jean in 1788. For example:

> Farewell, thou stream that winding flows
>   Around Eliza's dwelling;
> O mem'ry, spare that cruel throes
>   Within my bosom swelling.
> > ("Song—," K 405)

Why, we must wonder, did Burns write such dreadful songs just because Thomson wanted him to? Why did he put up with Thomson's bullying and execrable taste? And why did he give up the creative independence that he valued so much?

He received no money from Thomson, at his own insistence, although Thomson offered to pay him "any reasonable price." Burns said his songs were "either *above* or *below* price. . . . In the honest enthusiasm with which I embark in your undertaking, to talk of money, wages, fee, hire, &c. would be downright Sodomy of Soul" (R 507)! And Burns could have continued to publish his songs in *The Scots Musical Museum* without interference.

Cedric Thorpe Davie speculated that Burns's "enthusiasm for perpetuating the Scottish airs and widening the circles of those acquainted with them may have dimmed his judgment."[31] Thomson's *A Select Collection* was published in London and had a wider circulation than Johnson's *Scots Musical Museum.* But this explanation, while probably true in part, is not sufficient. The songs Burns published in *A Select Collection* were in a style that would do little to advance the cause of Scottish literature. Further explanation may come from Burns's statements and works.

It seems to me that Burns was losing his creative powers. He shows, in both his letters and his poetry, a confusion, a loss of direction, a search for a different style. Certainly his unfortunate circumstances— his poor health, money worries, demanding job, another illegitimate child—contributed to the problem. And Thomson deserves all the blame we can hang on him. But there is also some evidence of faltering in creativity.

Burns's letters to Thomson are full of self-contradiction. His first letter says: "Apropos, if you are for *English* verses, there is, on my part, an end of the matter.—Whether in the simplicity of *the Ballad,* or the pathos of *the Song,* I can only hope to please myself in being allowed at least a sprinkling of our native tongue" (R 507). Two-and-a-half years later, in a exasperated outburst, he writes: "These English songs gravel me to death.—I have not that command of the language that I have of my native tongue. In fact, I think my ideas are more barren in English than in Scotish. . . . I will vamp up the old Song & make it English enough to be understood" (R 644).

Burns seems not to know, even in his first letter to Thomson, whether he wants to write Scottish songs or English songs with a "sprinkling" of Scottish. In the later letter he has become understand-ably exasperated from writing English (read: neoclassical) songs. What he sends with this letter, however, are not Scottish songs that have been made "English enough to be understood," but deplorable third-rate imitations of early eighteenth-century English poets:

> Let not woman e'er complain
> Of inconstancy in love;
> Let not Woman e'er complain,
> Fickle Man is apt to rove. etc.

When Burns referred, in his letter, to his "barren" ideas, he meant what he said. In his letters in 1794 to people whose understanding far surpassed Thomson's, he is blunter. He writes to his other editor, James Johnson, connecting his low spirits, unfortunate circumstances, and lack of creativity: "I have, all this winter, been plagued with low spirits & blue devils, so that I have almost hung my harp on the wil-low-trees—" (R 616). And to his friend Alexander Cunningham, "For these two months I have not been able to lift a pen. My constitution

and frame were, *ab origine,* blasted with a deep incurable taint of hypochondria, which poisons my existence" (R 619).

His productivity appears to have been waning in many ways. He
rewrote some of the songs he had already published, often making
them worse (e.g., "How lang and dreary is the night"). He began
writing dreary odes (e.g., "Ode for General Washington's Birthday").
He wrote many bad poems during this period, more than he had in
previous years, and they are not all for Thomson's collection.

Some of the songs he wrote during these years are as good as he ever
wrote, but they occur less frequently and are in the same style as his
earlier ones. I can find no evidence of development. He wrote his two
songs on political freedom in these years, "Scots Wha Hae" and "Is
there for honest Poverty." But generally his subject matter is also
repetitious.

It is impossible to say what is cause and what is result. Burns's
creative powers may have been stifled by Thomson's pressures, or Burns
may have turned to Thomson because he felt his powers waning and
wanted direction. Or it could have been a combination. But it does
seem likely that the decline in the quality of his poetry in these last
years of his life was not solely due to Thomson's injurious influence.

It is not unusual for a poet to begin losing his creative powers in his
thirties or even younger. Wordsworth and Coleridge are examples. Perhaps the kind of poetry Burns had chosen to write in his songs, a poetry
of emotions, was the kind that is limited to young poets. It may be
that he had to move on or decline. Perhaps he would have developed
a new style had he lived—possibly in the manner of *Tam o'Shanter.* But
he had written *Tam o'Shanter* in 1790, and did not follow up on that
magnificent work. These years show no sign of future promise.

Not everything was bad in these last years. His reputation continued
to grow, in Scotland and abroad. He continued, until the end of 1794,
to write some exquisite lyrics. He took genuine pleasure in his family
and in his remaining friends. The situation was mixed, as it was in
most of his life, and this was a bad period. But it had its gratifications.

Burns died in July 1796, from some form of rheumatic fever or
endocarditis. Early biographers, eager to feel morally superior to
Burns, attributed his death to alcoholism, venereal disease, or general
debauchery. Physicians have more recently gone over the records and
demonstrated, fairly conclusively, that he died from a heart condition
that probably resulted from overwork on the farm at a young age.[32]

The development of his style, from "Holy Willie's Prayer" to "A red, red rose," is astonishing when we consider that his productive period lasted only ten years, and much of that time was taken up by farm work, work in the excise, and illness. The performance is impressive when viewed by itself or as an expression of his personal life. It becomes more impressive when seen as part of his age.

He lived most of his life in a Scottish village, but he was distinctly a man of his age in Britain. The literary and philosophical trends in Britain strongly influenced him. And he eloquently expressed the age's particular conflicts and ideals. It is, then, in the context of the late eighteenth century that we can most fully appreciate Burns's contribution as a poet.

Chapter Four

Burns and the Late Eighteenth Century

The Age of Burns

Understanding Burns's relationship to the late eighteenth century requires something not easy to come by, a definition of the period itself. The nineteenth- and early twentieth-century critics and literary historians called the period "pre-Romantic." Burns was its greatest writer, the poet who saved British poetry from the ice age of Augustanism. He was "born in an age the most prosaic Britain had yet seen"[1] and "restored passion to our poetry."[2] When mid-twentieth-century critics reevaluated and redeemed early eighteenth-century poetry, they ignored most of the second half of the century. The critics saved Johnson and Boswell by creating an "Age of Johnson" and saved Blake by pushing him forward into Romanticism. But Burns, along with Sterne, Cowper, and others, became awkwardly superfluous.

For T. S. Eliot, Burns was not a "pre-Romantic" but a "decadent representative of a great alien tradition."[3] For W. K. Wimsatt and Cleanth Brooks he was one of the "fake primitives or bourgeois poseurs."[4] David Daiches and John Speirs argued that he was not part of his age in Britain but was in a purely Scottish tradition.[5] Eliot, Wimsatt, and Brooks deal with Burns by putting him into some special class, Daiches and Speirs by hermetically sealing him off from the period he lived in. Most mid-twentieth-century critics had little patience with writers who did not fall into neatly defined traditions.

The late eighteenth century is an age for writers who do not easily fit into periodization. It was a time of enormous upheaval and uncertainty, so that its writers were especially experimental, volatile, and individualistic. An astonishing number of them—Collins, Smart, Cowper—were literally mad. Others, like Blake and Gray, were thought to be mad and did behave in bizarre ways. Johnson, Boswell, and Sterne wrote works that do not fit easily into the usual genres. While many writers clustered around Johnson, others, such as Gray, Cowper, and Blake, were largely isolated from other writers of the time. The age is not easily defined, but this lack of definition is part of its character.

Recently, some historians have begun to recognize the distinctiveness of the age,[6] and others have begun to treat Burns's writings in relation to his contemporaries.[7] The time has now come to see him as a member of the period he was so obviously a part of. He was outside the mainstream and so was well fitted for the task of creating a style of poetry appropriate for this confused, exhilarating age.

The late eighteenth century in Britain was the period in which it finally became clear that the old ethical and aesthetic systems could not comfortably be relied on to guide a person's behavior, that people had to begin to strike out on their own. The ideals that people had striven to live by, or at least pretended to strive for, changed in radical ways. The result was stimulating and frightening.

Political, moral, and aesthetic principles had remained reasonably consistent over the previous centuries. Most people believed that Christianity should govern morality and that hereditary government should enforce laws and maintain order. In the family, parents had the right to regulate the lives of their children in almost every respect. Between the sexes, men had most of the legal and moral regulation of their wives and unmarried daughters. The individual tried to follow his reason, which he believed would guide him in the direction that Christianity and tradition decreed. Artists and writers followed, in varying degree, the great synthesis of Christian and classical ideas and forms that had been developing since the late Middle Ages.

In politics, a struggle had been going on for centuries in most European countries between the king and the landed aristocracy and gentry, but no one questioned the ideas that the power should be in one or the other camp or in some combination of them. Now, in the second half of the eighteenth century, some people questioned whether power should reside entirely in either. The questioners, throughout the Western world, varied from radicals who argued for universal suffrage to moderates who wanted a slight expansion of the power base. The French and American revolutions were the most dramatic expression of this idea, but they were not the only serious challenges to hereditary government. For the first time in millennia, a widespread argument was being made that the power of government should be extended to other groups than royalty and landowners. The radical idea of human equality was beginning to be taken seriously.

In religion, most of Europe had been arguing for centuries over what was the true form of Christianity, but few questioned the ideal of Christianity in some form. Now, although few people advocated the abolishment of Christianity, many had questions about it and agonized about it. Others showed indifference, simply not considering it very seriously as a source of ethical guidance. Writers, alternately stimulated and frightened by this new, apparent liberation from the ethical principles that had governed human behavior for centuries, sought to develop alternatives or attempt to reinterpret the ancient truths in terms of new kinds of experience.

And belief in miracles, superstitions, the Devil—the whole world of the supernatural and the irrational—was under attack. But these beliefs, like Christianity, were not ready to die. Writers of the Enlightenment mounted a formidable attack on phenomena that cannot be scientifically demonstrated. But established beliefs die slowly, and most thoughtful people were uncertain about what to believe.

Concurrent with the new sense of liberation, other structures of power, especially the family, came in for reconsideration. In the past, grown children may have had some veto power over whom they should marry and, in the case of male children, what career to follow, but they had few other rights. Now, there was some questioning of parental authority. The challenge was less serious than the challenge to king, aristocracy, and church. The family was obviously still intact and had probably been made stronger in Britain by Protestantism. But writers were beginning to debate whether parents always know best and to suggest that some parents may be tyrannical. The thoughts and feelings of children received new attention.

The rights of women began to be discussed. Some people argued for more education for women, for increased legal rights for wives, or for allowing mothers more control in raising children. A few fortunate women actually got an improved education. Women began to speak out, and some women made a living by writing novels. Women started to appear more frequently at the center of literary works. And in the last decade of the century, Mary Wollstonecraft argued for equality for women. Wollstonecraft's stunningly courageous writings had little immediate influence. But they provided powerful evidence of how seriously the issue was being discussed.

The hierarchy inside the self was challenged. In the past, most good writers and thinkers acknowledged that we do not always follow reason and that emotions are to be valued. But the desirability of giving reason the greater control of our actions was rarely questioned. Donne had called reason the "viceroy of God." Pope had said: "On life's vast ocean diversely we sail, / Reason the card, but Passion is the gale" (*Essay on Man,* 2.107–8). Now, many writers began to wonder whether passion might not be the better "card" for some parts of life. Only a few now argued for total surrender to the emotions, but the emotions were elevated and given greater respect.

Literary forms and styles demonstrate the new sense of freedom. The "rules" that Burns and others railed against—the principles developed out of a synthesis of Renaissance critical ideas with those of Aristotle, Horace, Longinus, and others—had never taken a strong hold in Britain. Yet the presence of a classical ideal, a synthesis of classical and Christian ideas, an admiration for classical forms, and a rich use of classical mythology and history had been powerful forces in the style of British literature for centuries. Some of the greatest writers in British literature had followed the classical forms of tragedy, epic, pastoral, georgic, and satire.

In the earlier half of the century, the influence of classical forms was obviously weakening. Pope, Swift, and Gay wrote mock-epics, mock-georgics, and mock-pastorals as if to say that the age could not support the noble forms. Pope and other theorists cautioned against excessive adherence to the rules, but they acknowledged them and respected them. A sense of classicism, a respect for Augustan Rome, was still evident.

In the latter half, the traditional forms were not often used, even ironically. Instead, from the 1740s onward, the literary scene was marked by experimentation. The psychological novel was developed. Works dealing with details of daily life—biography, autobiography, journals—became common. Poets experimented with Greek forms (as opposed to the more traditional Roman ones). Medieval or pseudomedieval styles and subjects were used. Songs were treated more seriously. After Johnson's "Vanity of Human Wishes," satire became chatty, more good humored, less prescriptive.

Simple life and simple styles were extolled more than in the past and in a different form. Early in the century, Addison had admired the "beautiful simplicity" and "natural way of writing" of the ancients,[8] by which he meant a kind of refined classicism, an avoidance of baroque complexity. He meant something different from Joseph Warton who, in mid-century, said he would "rather sit in the grotto of Calypso than in the most pompous saloon of Louis XV."[9] Poetically, the belief in simplicity appeared in such subjects as Gray asking no more than a simple tombstone in a country churchyard or Cowper wandering in the woods. Classical mythological references gave way to nature images. Commonplace images were no longer treated ironically. The polished heroic couplet gave way to blank verse, the irregularity of the ode, and the simple meters and rhyme schemes of the song.

Literary theorists extolled what was original, by which they meant works that did not follow established classical forms or retell, in the classical and Renaissance manner, historical or mythological subjects or old tales. Augustan theorists had recommended that poets follow some degree of original creativity. But now terms like "pleasure of the imagination" and "exuberance of fancy" appear at the center of critical thought. Writers were more on their own, no longer with models, rules, and forms to guide them. Their style and their subjects supposedly came out of their observations, experiences, and emotions.

Burns was in an especially good position to understand and develop these new ideas and to create a new style that would express them. Because the Scots had a long tradition of egalitarianism,[10] he was prepared for the new democratic ideas. As a member of a divided church he had developed some perspective on the concept of organized religion. As an economically oppressed farmer and as a citizen of an oppressed country, he had developed suspicion of authority and the state. As a man who was self-educated and had read the writers of the Enlightenment, he was familiar with the new ideas that were challenging the old concepts of state and religion; as someone who lived most of his life in a small, rustic village, he had close touch with the common stream of life.

Because he was a farmer, a man of little formal education, a Scotsman, he could write about the simple life, about the denial of old forms. Since Calvinism discouraged ceremony,[11] he was familiar with a certain austere aesthetics. His poverty had made practical simplicity a necessity, so he could use subject matter and imagery that openly reflected his experience. He could write about daily life from the real simplicity of a farm, not from the fake simplicity of Calypso's grotto.

A Poet of Democracy

Burns made theoretical observations about poetry in his letters and journals. His favorable comments on "pastoral simplicity," the "wild," the "irregular," the "natural," and the "spontaneous language of my heart"; and his dislike of "scientific criticism," "Greek and Roman appelations," and "Darts, flames, Cupids, loves, graces, and all that farrago" are commonplaces for his age that can be found throughout mid-century criticism. And many poets, such as Cowper and Goldsmith, followed these principles, writing in a plainer style than the Augustan poets. They used less Latinate diction, simpler images, more familiar subjects. Their verse form was blank verse or heroic couplets softened with numerous run-on lines.

Burns, however, seems to be especially effective in translating the simple style into an expression of the democratic ideals of his period. The poet who has "to Laerning nae pretence," the farmer who feels kinship with his old mare, the beggars who can find joy in camaraderie in a country inn, the portrayal of ordinary emotions in a simple peasant girl are all expressions of respect for all people, concrete examples of democratic thinking. His recognition that the young women speaking in "Tam Glen" and "O Whistle and I'll come to ye my lad" deserve respect when they want to marry men whom their parents disapprove of, the respect for ordinary labor in "O Merry hae I been" and the epistles, all follow his belief in the special worth of every person.

Burns does not portray the poor as humble but happy, as does Gray, nor in an almost uninterrupted state of leisure, as does Goldsmith. He does not see them as people who are merely preferable to the spoiled rich, as does Cowper, nor as people who deserve our pity but not our respect, as does Crabbe.[12] Burns's rustics work hard, and they are often very poor. But they endure, and, although they may be comic at times, they are never pitiful. Perhaps only in Blake's portrayal of the urban poor, and even there to a lesser degree, do we find that combination of realism and respect for the masses that is the literary counterpart of democratic political theory.[13]

Burns has often been regarded as a poet of the people. A recent, intriguing illustration of this universal touch is his popularity in China.[14] His ability to reach so wide an audience comes from his sense of the texture of the lives of ordinary people, from his ability to get into the minds of ordinary people and to see things from their point of view.

One example of this democratic sensibility is his treatment of women in his songs. Women are allowed to express a range of desires and problems, to speak for themselves without blame or guilt. They can express sexual desire as freely and openly as men, without being portrayed, as they often are in literature, as the sexually insatiable daughters of Eve tempting men to their downfall. Burns portrays their sexual desires with sympathy and with the amusement that such desires in either gender usually evokes; for example:

> Commend me to the Barn yard,
>> And the Corn-mou, man;   *pile of corn*
> I never gat my Coggie fou   *cup full*
>> Till I met wi' the Ploughman.
>>> ("The Ploughman," K 205)

> Wha will crack to me my lane;   *talk to me alone*
> Wha will mak me fidgin fain;   *tingle all over*
> Wha will kiss me o'er again,
> The rantin dog the Daddie o't.
>> ("The rantin dog," K 80)

Young women are allowed to express their fear of sex, as in "I'm o'er young to Marry Yet" (K 195), and to complain if they get stuck with an old husband, as in "What can a young lassie do wi' an auld man" (K 347).

Burns often portrays an unmarried pregnant woman as the victim of biology and an unfair social system. "The day it is short and the night it is lang, / The dearest siller [silver] that ever I wan [won]" ("The Taylor fell thro' the bed," K 286). "But Oh! I fear the kintra [country] soon / Will ken as weel's mysel!" ("To the Weaver's gin ye go," K 194) and:

> When a' the lave gae to their play,   *others*
> Then I maun sit the lee-lang day,   *must; live-long*
> And jeeg the cradle wi' my tae   *jog*
>> And a' for the bad girdin o't.   *shoving or riding*
>>> ("Duncan Gray," K 204)

The women do not passively accept their suffering or internalize their oppression. The pregnant women assert their resentment directly and energetically: "Weary fa you, [damn you] Duncan Gray" ("Duncan Gray," K 204) and "But deevil damn the lousy loun, [lout] / Denies the bairn [child] he got" ("Wha'll m———w me now," K 613).

Burns, once again, has drawn on his familiarity with the English literary tradition and the Scottish folk tradition. In the eighteenth century Defoe, Pope, and Richardson had begun a serious examination of the conditions imposed on women. Women novelists of the century, such as Ann Radcliffe and Frances Burney, often created strong, relatively independent heroines.[15] On the other hand, Scottish folk songs often express a down-to-earth acceptance of sexuality for women as well as men. And, as one historian suggests, lower-class women may have had greater sexual equality than their social superiors.[16]

Burns combined the new feminism with the racy style of folk songs to create songs that speak from a woman's standpoint, that give them genuine dignity. In his songs, women are not wept over, as in Pope's "Elegy to the Memory of an Unfortunate Lady" and Richardson's *Clarissa,* or made to fade away quietly in melancholy and guilt, as in Goldsmith's "When lovely woman stoops to folly":

> The only art her guilt to cover,
>   To hide her shame from every eye,
> To give repentance to her lover,
>   And wring his bosom, is—to die.

Burns's ability to understand the plight of the oppressed even allows him to describe the situation of a prostitute whose pregnancy interferes with her livelihood:

> O wha'll m———w me now, my jo,
>   An' wha'll m———w me now:
> A sodger wi' his bandileers   *ammunition box*
>   Has bang'd my belly fu'.
> . . . .
> Our dame can lae her ain gudeman,   *own husband*
>   An' m———w for glutton greed;
> An' yet misca's a young thing   *scolds*
>   That's m———n' for its bread.
> ("Wha'll m———w me now," K 613)

Burns was not as consistent as we might like. He could be brutal ("Epistle to J.R.******," K 47 and "The Trogger," K 610) and pa-tronizing ("The Rights of Women," K 390). In *Tam o'Shanter* he pre-sents Tam's wife, Kate, as the stereotype of female repressiveness of male freedom. Still, Burns, more than any other writer before Woll-stonecraft, examined a range of women's problems and strengths, showed respect for unmarried pregnant women, and recognized that a prostitute had to "mow" for her bread. He did not apologize for these women, convert them to Christian repentance, or hurriedly marry them off to any man who would have them. Instead, he let them speak for themselves with independence and force.

His sympathy and vigorous expression of the condition of women is one example of his understanding of the condition of people outside the mainstream of literature. In the breadth of his description of the living conditions, the social conditions, the thoughts, and the feelings of women, peasants, beggars, and other oppressed groups; in his gen-uine respect for all decent human feelings; and in his concrete sense of the rich human implications of democratic ideals Burns stands out from all other writers of the late eighteenth century as a poet of democracy.[17]

The Uses of Autobiography

But what happens when you turn towards your inner self without the ethical guidance of religion or tradition? Burns's democratic poetry received some political direction from the ideas that were being ex-pressed throughout the western world in theory and in action. But when creative writers turned inward, to their own values, they found few principles to show them the way. They had to find it on their own.

In mid-century the good writers were aware of the new moral un-certainty but either accepted it or withdrew from it. Johnson put his acceptance into Christian terms, advocating "Obedient passions, and a will resign'd" ("Vanity of Human Wishes," 1.359). Other writers chose melancholy as a counterpart or an expression of religious uncertainty. Night and the graveyard became popular symbols. Gray was content when a ploughman left him in a "world of darkness" and concluded that "The paths of glory lead but to the grave" ("Elegy Written in a Country Churchyard"). In the graveyard, said Collins, "*Freedom* shall a-while repair, / To dwell a weeping Hermit there" ("Ode, *Written in the Beginning of the Year* 1746"). Blair wrote *The Grave* and Young wrote *Night Thoughts on Life, Death, and Immortality.* [18]

In the last four decades of the century, however, writers began to emerge from this quiet acceptance and gloomy denial. They began to seek a new kind of guidance. Some sought a moral direction that would be more consistent with the energy generated by the optimism of the Enlightenment and the hopefulness of contemporary politics. Others seemed to sink more deeply into gloom but, unable to find consolation in Johnsonian acceptance, continued to search for other answers. This new search shows up most strikingly in a new kind of autobiographical writing.

Jean Hagstrum, referring to Rousseau's *Confessions,* says that at this period "the spirit of man must fall back upon itself without external guides and sanctions and cut its own path through the jungles of individual and social passion." [19] In Britain, in the same period, in the autobiographical and semi-autobiographical writings of Burns (the epistles), Cowper (*The Task*), Sterne (*Tristram Shandy* and *A Sentimental Journey*), and Boswell (the various journals), we can find some counterparts to Rousseau's *Confessions.* These works are not formal autobiographies, and they all contain some fictional or dramatic elements. But they also convey the sense of the writer himself, examining whole passages of his life, attempting to cut his "own path through the jungles of individual and social passion."

These works lack a clearly explicated moral purpose. Earlier autobiographical writers set out to prove a point, usually that some critical event occurred that changed the writers' lives and turned them back to God. But, as Fredric Bogel says, "What distinguishes the major autobiographical writers of the later eighteenth century . . . is precisely the disappearance . . . of such moments." [20] The new autobiographical works follow the experiences of the author in an apparently spontaneous, disordered sequence that is subject to chance. The writers give the sense that they are describing events as they occur and letting them prove what they may. The emphasis shifts from the moral purpose to the individual moment.

Late eighteenth-century writers often expressed this new kind of experience through the metaphor of unstructured wandering. When wandering occurred in earlier literature, the wanderers were lost or exiled. No one just set out with the intention of wandering as an end in itself. If people went for a walk, they took a direct and defined path.

Now they begin to wander, footloose, more concerned with what happens to them along the way than with the place they are going to. Sterne goes on a sentimental journey, not on the Grand Tour.

Images of wandering began to appear early in the eighteenth century, notably in Thomson's *The Seasons*. Thomson used the image as an expression of the freedom of an unstructured life: "Shall we wind / Along the streams? or walk the smiling mead? / Or court the forest glades? or wander wild?" (*Summer,* ll. 1403–5). But he never goes beyond description. At most, his wandering allows him to enjoy nature: "Oft let me wander o'er the dewy fields / Where freshness breathes" (*Spring,* ll. 103–4). Or to learn from it: "Here wandering oft . . . / [I] meditate the book / Of Nature, ever open" (*Autumn,* ll. 669–71).

Cowper goes further. In *The Task* he used the image repeatedly to express his loss of direction, as for example, in poetry

> As one who, long in thickets and in brakes
> Entangled, winds now this way and now that
> His devious course uncertain, seeking home.
> . . . .
> So I designing other themes,
> . . . .
> Have rambled wide.
>
> (3.1–14)

And his moral and psychological loss of direction:

> I was a stricken deer, that left the herd
> . . . .
> Since then, with few associates, in remote
> And silent woods I wander.
>
> (3.108–18)

At times his wandering seems to be hopeless: "Roving as I rove, / Where shall I find an end, or how proceed?" (4.232–33). But at other times he lets his mind wander, to find "pleasures" in "The thoughtful or unthinking mind, / The mind contemplative" (4.279–80). At still other times he combines his fancy (or imagination) with love of nature to find some meaning in it and in dreams:

> There early stray'd
> My fancy, ere yet liberty of choice
> Had found me, or the hope of being free.
> My very dreams were rural.
>
> (4.697–700)

And he finds "comfort of a reasonable joy" in "spirits buoyant with excess of glee," in contemplation of the "wanton" horse, and "The very kine that gambol at high noon" (6.329–47).

The Task was printed after Burns had written but not published most of his epistles, so there could have been no direct influence either way. Yet Burns uses images and themes that are strikingly similar to Cowper's. He combines wandering in nature with imagination, the creation of poetry, and self-examination. But his vision is happier than Cowper's:

> The *Muse* nae *Poet* ever fand her,
> Till by himsel he learn'd to wander,
> Adown some trottin burn's meander,
>   An' no think lang;
> O sweet, to stray an' pensive ponder
>   A heart-felt sang.
> ("To W. S*****n, Ochiltree," ll. 85–90, K 59)

The poet can "stray an' pensive ponder," but he must also "no think lang." That is, he can muse over ideas so long as he does it in a subjective, unstructured way, in a way that is like the meandering of the stream. And the "pensive ponder" is balanced by the emotions of "sweet" and "heart-felt." The "heart-felt sang" will come to the poet who allows himself to be led by both thought and feeling (but more by the latter).

"To J.S****" (K 79), as we have noted, is organized around the contrast between Burns, who wanders, roams, frisks, rhymes "for fun," and the "douse folk," who "live by rule" and "ken the road." His other epistles are not so specifically structured around that metaphor, but almost all use some images of wandering or unordered movement: "We wander out, we know not where," ("Epistle to Davie," K 51) and "Then, hiltie, skiltie, we gae scrivin' [gliding along]" ("Second Epistle to Davie," K 101). Pope, in *An Essay on Man,* had described "this scene of Man" as a "mighty maze! but not without a plan." For Burns it is not a maze, and it is without a plan. Burns says that there is no order except what we can derive from our own feelings, which we can sense most vividly when we forget the road and concentrate on our sensations as we ramble.

Cowper finds consolation and comfort by wandering "pensive" in the "groves" and subjecting himself, half-thinking, to the "the moon-beam," and "the sleeping leaves" (1.761–63). Christianity sometimes eases his despair. The nature that he wanders in, "the beauties of the wilderness," present "A soul in all things, and that soul is God" (4.185–86). But just as often he must wander in "devious course uncertain, seeking home." His despair is not complete, but it is so vividly described that it will not entirely disappear from our memory: "From slough to slough / Plunging and half despairing of escape" (3.3–6). Burns is also divided, but between thought and feeling, by pensively pondering a "heart-felt sang," by thinking but not "lang," by watching the "never-halting moments" with "tentless heed." Christianity for Cowper and emotions for Burns offer the stronger direction, but neither force quite triumphs.[21]

Burns used the unplanned creative act as an example of the spontaneous life. Here he is closer to Sterne's prose than to Cowper's poetry. (And here there is the possibility of direct influence.)[22] Sterne and Burns both write as if they do not plan the work they are writing, that the work itself is left to chance. Sterne, for example, says, "All my heroes are off my hands;—'tis the first time I have had a moment to spare,—and I'll make use of it, and write my preface" (*Tristram Shandy*, 3:20). He wonders aloud what he is going to write next: "But where am I going? these reflections croud in upon me ten pages at least too soon, and take up that time which I ought to bestow upon facts" (*Tristram Shandy*, 6:29).

Burns also wonders aloud:

> But how the subject theme may gang,   *go*
>   Let time and chance determine;
> Perhaps it may turn out a Sang;
>   Perhaps turn out a Sermon.
> ("Epistle to a Young Friend," ll. 5–8, K 105)

> Sae I've begun to scrawl, but whether
> In rhyme, or prose, or baith thegither,   *both together*

Or some hotch-potch that's rightly neither,
    Let time mak proof;   *make*
But I shall scribble down some blether   *babble*
    Just clean aff-loff.   *offhand*
        ("To the Same," ll. 37–42, K 58)

And Burns makes Sterne's "reflections croud in upon me" even more vivid: "The words come skelpan, [rushing] rank and file, / Amaist before I ken! ("Epistle to Davie," ll. 142–43, K 51).

    Both Sterne and Burns give themselves over to an inner, instinctual guide that operates without their conscious control. Sterne relinquishes the conscious choice of where to place the preface. Burns allows "time and chance" to determine whether his poem turns out to be lyrical or moral; and to let time "mak proof" whether his "scrawl" is "rhyme, or prose." Sterne's "reflections croud in" on him. The action of Burns's "skelpin" words is near to preconscious: "Amaist before I ken."

    Sterne struggles to write: "All I fret and fume at, and what most distresses my invention at present, is how to bring the point itself to bear" (*Tristram Shandy,* 3:20). Burns also struggles. But he uses his muse and Pegasus to describe the struggle within himself in more physically explicit terms than Sterne does: "My awkwart Muse sair pleads and begs, / I would na write ("To the Same," ll. 11–12, K 58). And:

My spavet *Pegasus* will limp,   *spavined*
    Till ance he's fairly het;   *once; hot*
And then he'll hilch, and stilt, and jimp,   *lurch; prance, jump*
    And rin an unco fit.   *run; strange*
    (Epistle to Davie," ll. 147–50, K 51)

Sterne and Burns both describe the familiar psychological phenomenon in which a person has trouble doing what he rationally wants to do because his irrational self wants to do something else. And both writers leave the conflict somewhat unresolved. The conscious side does win out, the work gets written. But the irrational drives get expressed too vividly to be dismissed, and the shape of the work is not entirely determined by the conscious will. The rational wins but is not victorious.

    Sterne and Burns created a style to convey this professed lack of control, to suggest that spontaneity or impulsiveness has the governance. Sterne uses innumerable devices to express spontaneity—changing subject in the middle of a chapter, apparent digressions, the use of the dash, etc. Burns conveys spontaneity by similar devices. For example, the short line of the Standard Habbie verse to throw in an afterthought or aside, as "E'en let them clash! [chatter]" or "Plain truth to speak."

Sterne thinks aloud. In one place he uses the amusingly old-fashioned device of moral personifications to express his rational self, and he uses irregular syntax to express his emotional self. He is debating whether to share his chaise with a lady whose hand he has been holding for an inordinately long time: "You know not who she is, said Caution—or what scrapes the affair may draw you into, whispered Cowardice—. . . .—But 'tis a civil thing, said I—and as I generally act from the first impulse, and therefore seldom listen to these cabals . . .—I instantly turned to the lady" (*Sentimental Journey,* "The Remise Door: Calais").

Burns will also interrupt the syntax to think aloud: "Whilst I—but I shall haud [hold] me there— / Wi' you I'll scarce gang [go] *ony where—*" ("To J.S****," K 79, ll. 169–70); and:

> Eve's bonie Squad, Priests wyte them sheerly,   *blame*
>   For our grand fa':
> But still—but still—I like them dearly:
>   God bless them a'!
>   ("Epistle to Captain William Logan
>   at Park—," K 129)

Boswell joins the public ambivalence in his notorious moral waverings. One day he "took the first whore I met. . . . I had a low opinion of this gross practice and resolved to do it no more." A few days later, "I met with a monstrous big whore in the Strand, whom I had a great curiosity to lubricate. . . . She would by no means take what I offered her. . . . I walked off with the gravity of a Barcelona bishop. . . . I was so much in the lewd humor that I felt myself restless, and took a little girl into a court; but wanted vigor. So I went home, resolved against low street debauchery" (*London Journal,* 31 March and 13 April 1763).

In these passages all three writers express their moral ambivalence (in this case the conflict between moral dictates and sexual interest) by thinking aloud. The conflict may or may not be resolved, but it becomes more interesting than the resolution. Sterne's irreverent dismissal of the old moral strictures, Boswell's marvelous indifference to his own inconsistency, and Burns's hesitant but determined rejection of church values describe a new element in literature. Earlier literature, starting with Homer and the Bible, of course discusses moral uncertainty, procrastination, and divided motivation. What is new with Burns, Sterne, and Boswell is that they openly, cheerfully, stylistically, and thematically express and accept the conflict. The expression of the struggle takes precedence over the attempt at resolution.

Samuel Johnson, a decade before Sterne started writing, had described the pain of procrastination in *Rambler* 134: "To act is far easier than to suffer, yet we every day see the progress of life retarded by the *vis inertiae*, the mere repugnance to motion, and find multitudes repining at the want of that which nothing but idleness hinders them from enjoying." Johnson is closer to Sterne and Burns than he is to many older moralists. He invokes none of the standard moral proscriptions against the sin of sloth. But the pain, exquisitely described, is evident throughout the essay. Procrastination is understandable to Johnson, but it is still a great burden.

Procrastination and other moral conflicts create much less of a burden for the younger writers. Sterne and Burns, who simply accept the uncertainty, are more comfortable with such conflicts than are Cowper and Boswell. Sterne cheerfully relinquishes control over the direction of his work and his moral decisions. Burns seems proud and pleased that his Pegasus will "rin an unco fit," that his conscious control will not determine whether he writes a song or a sermon, that he likes "Eve's bonie squad" in spite of priestly admonition. The conflicts that, for millennia, writers had either resolved, or tried very hard to resolve, or recommended resolving, now come into the open, unresolved, unashamed, even glorified. In Burns and Sterne the ancient belief in reason as a way to control man's sinful nature has given way to the modern belief that many moral conflicts cannot be resolved and do not need to be.

Earl Wasserman has argued that such divisions in the late eighteenth century prevented the age from developing a "poetic syntax." "It also is a confession that the age could not hold the world together and that everyone was of the Shandy household."[23] Certainly Burns, Boswell, and even Cowper seem at times to be characters out of *Tristram Shandy*.

But their very styles create a kind of poetic syntax. They have fixed, in print, modern irresolution and have demonstrated that one can live with it and even enjoy it.[24]

Earlier, I quoted Pope's couplet: "On life's vast ocean diversely we sail, / Reason the card, but Passion is the gale." In Sterne and Burns the card is no longer reason's. Nor is it a combination of reason and passion—that solution would be what Pope said originally. Sterne and Burns have instead opened themselves to use and respond to whatever card comes to hand.

These writers use the description of minute, interior sensations to offer ethical or aesthetic guidance. For example:

—In doing this, [toasting the King of France] I felt every vessel in my frame dilate—the arteries beat all chearily together. (*Sentimental Journey*, "Calais")

> There was *ae sang,* amang the rest,
> . . . .
> It thirl'd the heart-strings thro' the breast,   *pierced*
>   A' to the life
> . . . .
> It pat me fidgean-fain to hear't.   *tickle all over*
> ("Epistle to J.L*****k," ll. 13–18, & 25, K 57.)

> At Wallace' name, what Scottish blood,
> But boils up in a spring-tide flood!
> ("To W.S*****n, Ochiltree," ll. 61–62, K 59)

The writers say that whatever goes on inside a person, no matter how minute, is worth attention and respect. They express a kind of democracy of the body.[25]

Sterne and Burns go further than Boswell. All three have at times relinquished their mind's control over their actions and assigned its authority to the heart and occasionally to the loins. Now Sterne and Burns move the governance to the body at large. Sterne's toast to the King of France is sanctioned by the dilation of his vessels. Burns's high evaluation of Lapraik's poetry comes from its ability to make him "fidgean-fain" and to "fissle." His judgment is determined by the sensation of his bloodstream.

Burns and Sterne are writing in the benevolist tradition that says that since man is essentially good, he need rely only on his own feelings to do the right thing. In the sentimental novel, such as the one that Burns admired, Mackenzie's *The Man of Feeling,* the hero is forever doing the right thing on the basis of his instincts and sensations. The hero is an innocent, a man who does not need to learn moral distinctions—he is already good.[26]

Both Burns and Sterne understood the shallowness of such an evaluation of human character; but they also saw the truth contained in it. For them benevolism provided an assessment of mankind that was as tenable as the older belief in man's essential depravity, and as dependable for moral and aesthetic guidance as the restrictions of religion and critical rules. They use the same device as does the sentimental novel, that is, they depend on their sensations for guidance. But through humor and liveliness they have given an ironic slant to benevolism.

Where the heroes of the sentimental novels are unbearably solemn, Burns and Sterne are always joking, horsing around, never taking themselves or benevolism entirely seriously. And they maintain a certain balance in other ways as well. Burns likes "Eve's bonie squad," but he does not contradict the priests' blame. Sterne makes no apology for inviting the woman into his chaise, but he does not claim that his doing so is right or proper or even wise. Sterne makes himself sound faintly ridiculous when his arteries dilate over his toasting the King of France. Burns does not expect us to take his judgment of Lapraik's poetry, based on his tingling, as conclusive. He likes it, that's enough.

Burns adds the democratic belief that people deserve to be equal to the benevolist belief that people are good. So when he talks about himself and his feelings, he does so in a way that implies that he is talking about the importance of all people, even those outside the mainstream. The figure of the untutored poet-ploughman, for example, becomes an expression that is at once personal and political:

> What's a' your jargon o' your Schools,
> Your Latin names for horns an' stools;
> If honest Nature made you *fools,*
>   What sairs your Grammars?   *serves*
> Ye'd better taen up *spades* and *shools,*   *taken; shovels*
>   Or *knappin-hammers.*   *stone hammers*
>
> A set a dull, conceited Hashes,   *fools*
> Confuse their brains in *Colledge-classes!*
> They *gang in* Stirks, and *come out* Asses,   *young steer*

> Plain truth to speak;
> An' syne they think to climb Parnassus
> By dint o' Greek.
>
> Gie me ae spark o' Nature's fire,
> That's a' the learning I desire;
> Then tho' I drudge thro' dub an' mire
> At pleugh or cart,   *plough*
> My Muse, tho' hamely in attire,
> May touch the heart.
>   ("Epistle to J. L*****k," ll. 61–78,
>   K 57)

Sterne frequently said something similar, but Burns took the ideas further. When Sterne attacked pedantic rules and substituted natural inspiration, he spoke with the personality of an educated, sophisticated wit who knows the rules and has chosen to reject them: "Great *Apollo*! if thou art in a giving humour,—give me,—I ask no more, but one stroke of native humour, with a single spark of thy own fire along with it" (*Tristram Shandy*, 3.xii). Burns put the ideas into the words of a ploughman, in the setting of a farm. He says that the creative process is as accessible as the ability to work a plough. Everyone, even those who, like himself, must "drudge thro' dub an' mire," can be inspired by "Nature's fire" and can have a muse who is "hamely in attire." Everyone can "touch the heart." The denunciation of the "jargon o' your schools" goes beyond the age's denunciation of pedantic strictures and becomes an argument against class oppression. The praise of "Nature's fire" goes beyond the age's praise of natural inspiration and becomes an argument for the recognition of human equality.

The exuberance in the works of both Burns and Sterne, their acceptance both of themselves and of others, offers a new way to find moral guidance. They go beyond the acceptance and enjoyment of moral conflict to see their sensations as moral guides. Cowper and Boswell follow their sensations but are at times uncertain about the wisdom of doing so. For Burns and Sterne, the need to resolve conflicts about religious belief, aesthetic principles, work, and sexual desire are no longer troublesome problems. Celebration of the moment, of the emotions, of spontaneity, of the creative act, of the sense of self, and of the common sympathy for all people has become the new morality.

This moral code is not as absolute nor as reliable as Christianity claims to be. And the doctrine of benevolism must be seen as limited by inevitable human weakness. But so long as we take benevolism and reliance on feelings with some irony and lightheartedness, they will help us to live our lives morally, meaningfully, and in freedom. Sterne and Burns have tempered the doctrine of benevolism, and Burns has added the belief of democracy, and they have created a new ethic of exuberant human liberation.

The Love of Place and Nature

The exuberance, freedom, and liberation not surprisingly led to a need for some kind of stability somewhere. In Burns it led to a love of place, love for his country of Scotland and for his native county of Ayrshire. And it led to a love of nature, which Burns combined with the love for his own land.

Scotland represented, for Burns, independence from England, and by extension, freedom from oppression. It also encouraged in him the nationalist fervor that was emerging in England and elsewhere in Europe. In England, patriotic songs and poems were popular. "God save Great *George* our king," which would become "God Save the King," appeared around the middle of the century. Henry Fielding wrote "The Roast Beef of Old England" with lines like: "Then, *Britons,* from all nice Dainties refrain, / Which effeminate *Italy, France,* and *Spain*; / And mighty Roast Beef shall command on the Main." And James Thomson, a native Scot who chose to live in England, wrote "Rule Britannia" with its refrain: "Rule, *Britannia,* rule the waves; / *Britons* never will be slaves."

Burns's patriotic poetry sounded a similar theme for Scotland. He presented it also as the country of freedom:

> Wha for Scotland's king and law,
> Freedom's sword will strongly draw,
> Free-man stand, or Free-man fa',
>   Let him follow me.
>   ("Scots, wha hae," K 425)

And it is a country, like Fielding's England, made strong by its no-nonsense simplicity:

> O Scotia! my dear, my native soil!
>   For whom my warmest wish to Heaven is sent!

Long may the hardy sons of *rustic toil*
   Be blest with health and peace and sweet content!
("The Cotter's Saturday Night," ll. 172–75, K 72)

But in spite of the popularity of "Scots wha hae," Burns did not write many nationalistic poems. And he did not, as we have noted, usually follow the Scottish nationalist idealization of the Jacobite past. Nor did he often go along with another popular trend, the contemporary romanticization of the Scottish Highlands.

The Scottish Highlands had begun to appear, in mid-century English poetry, as a symbol of what was strange and intriguing, as in Collins's "An Ode on the Popular Superstitions of the Highlands of Scotland." This interest was part of a general search for the exotic in unknown or primitive places and times—Wales, Persia, the Middle Ages, preclassical Greece. And Scotland's place in this array of exotica was emphasized by the contemporary attention given to the fake epic poetry that James Macpherson pretended to have discovered. His claim, that he had found the long lost work of an ancient Scottish bard, Ossian, set the intelligentsia of Europe agog. Burns paid some occasional lip service to Ossian but generally ignored him.

Burns admired the freedom and simplicity of the Highland life and often praised the Highlandmen for their independence and courage. But he also saw the Highlands as "a country where savage streams tumble over savage mountains, thinly overspread with savage flocks, which starvingly support as savage inhabitants" (R 116). Burns was never much interested in those sublime or mysterious subjects that were popular during his age. And, while he never says so, he apparently rejected the obviously patronizing implications of the·English fascination with the primitive Highlands. Burns interest here, as always, was with the familiar human experience. In this instance, the familiar was the natural scenes of Scotland viewed without rapture.

In writing about the natural scenes of Scotland, Burns was in the eighteenth-century tradition of nature poetry such as appeared in the works of Thomson and Cowper. Nature became in the works of the three poets more than a setting or a source of symbolism. The poet entered into the natural scene and stayed there. Nature became, especially in Thomson, the subject of the poem, not a backdrop or a symbol for something else.

Thomson's descriptions of the natural scene and of his responses to it are vivid and concrete, but are rarely located in a specific place. The location could be any where, as: "See how the lily drinks / The latent rill. . . . / Where the breeze blows from yon extended field / Of blossomed beans" ("Spring," ll.495–500). Burns is specific. As Robert Fergusson roots his poetry firmly in Edinburgh and other places in Scotland (e.g., *"Auld Reikie"* and *"Dumfries"*), Burns gives names of places, especially in his beloved county of Ayrshire:

> Ev'n winter bleak has charms to me,
> When winds rave thro' the naked tree;
> Or frosts on hills of *Ochiltree*
>   Are hoary grey;
> Or blinding drifts wild-furious flee,
>   Dark'ning the day!
> ("To W.S*****n, Ochiltree," ll.73–78, K 59)

Burns uses the sense of a specific place to evoke a range of emotions, developing the sense of place through the play on many physical senses. For example he uses the description of Afton, a small river in Ayrshire, to give his feeling for his love:

> How pleasant thy banks and green vallies below,
> Where wild in the woodlands the primroses blow;
> There oft as mild ev'ning weeps over the lea,
> The sweet scented birk shades my Mary and me.
>   ("Afton Water," K 257)

He will use the love of place and of nature to evoke nostalgia, as in songs of parting:

> But here alas! for me nae mair
>   Shall birdie charm, or floweret smile;
> Farewell the bonnie banks of Ayr,
>   Fareweel, fareweel! sweet Ballochmyle!
>   ("The Braes o' Ballochmyle," K 66)

Maynard Mack suggests that Burns's Ayrshire is like Pope's Twickenham Villa, "or Gray's playing fields of Eton . . . and Wordsworth's Lake Country. . . . the Arcadian impulse turns visibly more inward. It incorporates itself with that intensifying strain of self-consciousness and individualism that we associate with . . . Milton's 'paradise within thee happier far,' which is to compensate for the

lost garden."[27] But Burns creates only the faintest echo of the lost
Eden. He is closer to Gray's playing fields of Eton than to Milton's
paradise within, Pope's country of the mind, or Wordsworth's Lake
Country.

Christianity traditionally looked backward to Eden and forward to
heaven. In the late eighteenth century both paradises were often all but
forgotten. Boswell looked forward to his reward in this world, when
he could retire to Auchenleck, his family's estate, and enjoy the recollections of his extremely active life. As Boswell looked no further
forward than to his old age, so Gray looked no further backward than
to his childhood:

> Ah happy hills, ah pleasing shade,
> Ah fields belov'd in vain,
> Where once my careless childhood stray'd,
> A stranger yet to pain!
> ("Ode on a Distant Prospect of Eton College")

Burns, like Gray, does not seek a biblical past, even symbolically, just
as he does not pursue the political past of Jacobitism. The names of
"the bonnie banks of Ayr" and "sweet Ballochmyle" in "The Braes o'
Ballochmyle" firmly, insistently place his paradise in the realm of the
present and the familiar. His desired past is bounded and enriched by
his experience.

Burns does not always locate his nature imagery in a specific place.
In the English-speaking world's most most popular song of nostalgia
he uses generalized nature images to evoke a sense of the remembered
past:

> We two hae run about the braes,   *slopes*
>   And pou'd the gowans fine;   *daisies*
> But we've wandered mony a weary fitt,
>   Sin auld lang syne.   *since times long past*

Perhaps the extraordinary popularity of "Auld Lang Syne" (K 240)
as a song of recollection and hope in the modern world depends on its
associations, which are rooted in experience, familiar nature, and
earthly expectations. The song evokes, for the most secular of holidays,
the simple memories of childhood and old friendship. And it hopes for
no more than a future that offers a continuation of that friendship.

Burns wrote, in "Is there for Honest Poverty," one of the most popular British songs of political freedom. In "Auld Lang Syne" he came as close as anyone has to writing a universal secular hymn to earthly memories and expectations.[28]

The Paradox of Freedom

Songs lent themselves to subjects like love of pleasure, love of nature, earthly expectation, and respect for emotions but not to some of the other ideas that Burns had explored in his earlier poetry. For example, in *Love and Liberty* and in the epistles, he had examined the restrictions put on us emotionally, sexually, and artistically by religion and convention and had expressed the need to redefine morality in terms of sensation and energy. He had examined the question of knowledge and belief—how much we can accept the Enlightenment's belief in material proof and how much we can dismiss superstition—in "Halloween," "Death and Doctor Hornbook," and "Address to the Deil." These issues were important to late eighteenth-century thought and to Burns. But they were not issues easily discussed in songs.

William Blake, who was almost exactly contemporary with Burns, was struggling with these issues at the same time. These two poets are seldom compared,[29] although they came from similar social backgrounds, wrote and published much of their poetry at about the same time, and reflected similar influences and ideas. They were, to be sure, often unlike one another. But their similarities say something about the ideas of their age and their poetic expression.

Both Burns and Blake were men who were at home in a democratic and revolutionary age. They were "men of genius whose roots were in the common people."[30] Both attempted to write a kind of poetry that would be understandable to everyone. Both hated political repression and were sympathetic to the American and French revolutions, but they were distrustful of change through solely political means. Both hated religious repression, especially of sexual behavior, but remained believing Christians. Their disagreement was not with Christian ethics as they believed them to be revealed in the Bible. Rather, as Andrew Noble says, "they perceived human spontaneity and sexual vitality being devoured by a cancer of inverted spirituality, a Christless Christianity, the creation not of the divine but of the sick, repressed, and resentful!"[31] Both also hated the idea of rules in the arts and saw the strictures of neoclassicism as analogous to the oppressions of politics and the repressions of religion. And they both saw poetry and the creative imagination as expressions of personal freedom and as analogues to spiritual and sexual liberation.

They are at their most strikingly similar stylistically in their criticism of repression and spiritual sterility. For example, the strait and narrow road that Burns condemns throughout his epistles, the "road" that the "douse folk" "ken," is condemned by Blake in the "chartered street" and "chartered Thames" of "London." Burns's objection to arbitrary rules, "propriety's cold cautious rules," is expressed by Blake's "Jesus was all virtue and acted from impulse, not from rules." Both use the image of a standing pool to express the repressed psyches of what Burns calls the "unco guid" and what Blake calls "Prudence . . . a rich, ugly old maid." Blake says about such people, "Expect poison from the standing water." Burns says, "Your hearts are just a standing pool, / Your lives, a dyke."

Both explicitly condemn church and state as agents of repression, although in different tones:

> How the Chimney-sweeper's cry
> Every black'ning Church appalls,
> And the hapless Soldier's sigh
> Runs in blood down Palace walls.
>   ("London")

Burns's beggars sing their denunciation of church and court:

> A fig for those by law protected!
> Liberty's a glorious feast!
> Courts for Cowards were erected,
> Churches built to please the Priest.
>   (*Love and Liberty*)

Both, characteristic of their age, move away from satire to lyrical poetry. And both attempt to create new systems of ethics and knowledge. Their reinterpretation, independent of each other, of the Devil and the demonic provides an example of their ethical exploration.

In Burns's "Address to the Deil" (K 76), Satan is jocularly referred to as "Auld Hornie," who "Spairges about the brunstane cootie, [splashes about the brimstone wash basin] / To scaud poor wretches!" In the conclusion of the poem he addresses "auld *Cloots*":

> But fare you weel, auld *Nickie-ben!*
> O wad ye tak a thought an' men!   *mend*
> Ye aiblins might—I dinna ken—   *perhaps; don't know*
>   Still hae a *stake*—
> I'm wae to think upo' yon den,
>   Ev'n for your sake.

Burns's view is benevolist; he does not take the idea of sin very seriously. He hopes to convert the Devil, not to embrace him.

This poem was written in the winter of 1785–86. But a little over a year later Burns began referring to Milton's Satan as his "favourite hero" (R 113). In June he wrote: "I have bought a pocket Milton which I carry perpetually about with me, in order to study the sentiments— the dauntless magnanimity; the intrepid unyielding independence; the desperate daring, and noble defiance of hardship, in that great Personage, Satan" (R 114). This is possibly the first description of Milton's Satan as an admired hero.[32] Burns is expressing, through Satan, some of the revolutionary spirit of the age and some of his personal admiration for independence, daring, and defiance.

In *The Marriage of Heaven and Hell,* a few years later, Blake said something similar: "Note: The reason Milton wrote in fetters when he wrote of Angels & God, and at liberty when of Devils & Hell, is because he was a true Poet and of the Devil's party without knowing it." Blake's Devil represents the ideas that "The road of excess leads to the palace of wisdom" and "You never know what is enough unless you know what is more than enough." For both Blake and Burns, Milton's Devil stood for rebellion against unreasonable and repressive authority and for the freedom of the human spirit.

In *Tam o'Shanter* (K 321), written in 1790, Burns used the Devil and witches to explore the ideas of personal and aesthetic freedom, the limits of reason, and the defiance of established order in a way that is similar to Blake's statement in *The Marriage of Heaven and Hell* and in several poems from *Songs of Experience,* particularly "The Tyger." Both poets dealt with Satanic energy and the joy of excess. But Burns developed these subjects with a profound difference.

In *Tam o'Shanter* and "The Tyger" the poet relies on the contrast between a dark forest of the unknown and a blazing fire of emotional release. Both poems have a subject that is morally and emotionally ambiguous, and whose elusiveness is part of the statement. Both use a short rhyming couplet to intensify the emotion. And, most important,

in both poems the poets use the device of a speaker who is constricted
by reason and rules and who is disturbed by the energy and exuberance
of the poem's subject.[33] The speaker tries to force the subject into a
pattern where it will not fit. The result is a deeply affective tension
between the subject and the speaker that conveys some of the most
urgent topics of the age: the difficulty of handling emotional and sexual
energy in a world of social constraints; the difficulty of knowing what
is true and what is imagined in a world that has not defined a basis for
establishing knowledge; and the problem of writing in a world that
wants both uniform standards of communication and tolerance of spontaneity in artistic creation.

"The Tyger," as several modern commentators have noted, expresses
two points of view. The speaker is in a state of "self-induced fear"
created by his attempt to force the terrifying but exhilarating energy
of the tiger into a "frame." "The tone . . . is one of affrighted and
startled awe only if you dramatically attempt to project the poem's
speaker as the self-duped creature he assuredly is; read aloud with understanding, the tone has a fierce and ironic joy."[34] The speaker separates himself from the tiger by seeing the fire of its eyes in "distant
deeps and skies." The "fierce and ironic joy" comes from Blake's vision,
in which " 'The Tyger' is concerned with both the unprolific or dis-
torting and the truly creative process in spiritual life. . . . He is,
therefore, a creature to be confronted and contemplated not with un-
diluted fear but with that strange gaiety suggested by the visionary
intensity of the poem itself."[35] We see the tiger through both the constricted fear of the speaker and the fierce joy of Blake.

In *Tam o'Shanter* the speaker also tries to force the joy of Tam and
the energy of a wild witches' dance into the comfortable structure of a
rational, limited world. Burns has created a self-satisfied speaker who
wants, at times, to reduce everything to easily controlled or quantified
terms, such as conventional morality, facile nationalism, money, and
the neoclassical rules of poetry. But at other times he is less rigid and
enters into the joy of the poem. He "flits in and out of Tam's mind,
sometimes . . . seeing the world through Tam's eyes, sometimes seeing
Tam through his own."[36] He is "a man torn between Tam's values (the
pleasures of camaraderie, drink, sex, song, and dance) and Kate's
[Tam's wife's] values (respectability, responsibility, moral truths, and
Calvinistic rigor)."[37] Out of this double view of the speaker, Burns
creates a statement that transcends Tam's hedonism and Kate's
morality.

In the first twelve lines the speaker identifies himself with Tam. The pronouns are all "we," "our," and "us." Both he and Tam are in a tavern "bousing" and getting "unco happy," not thinking about the "lang Scots miles" and their "sulky sullen dame." Then at line thirteen they separate temporarily. Tam rides off, and the narrator pauses to lecture him. Burns used alliteration, feminine endings, and the strong beat of iambic tetrameter to convey the rhythm of someone who has incorporated Kate's moralistic fury: "She tauld thee weel thou was a skellum, [scoundrel] / A blethering, [chattering] blustering, drunken blellum [babbler]" (ll. 19–20). After thirty-two lines of moral outrage, the narrator pauses to philosophize for another four. He is made sad by the "mony lengthen'd sage advices, / The husband frae the wife despises," forgetting that he had been despising the same advice a few lines earlier. And then he returns to the tale he had almost forgotten:

> But to our tale: Ae market-night,
> *Tam* had got planted unco right;
> Fast by an ingle, bleezing finely,   *hearth; blazing*
> Wi' reaming swats, that drank divinely;   *beers*
> . . . .
> Kings may be blest, but *Tam* was glorious,
> O'er all the ills o' life victorious!
> (ll. 37–40; 57–58)

These lines are typical of the rhythm of the poem. Tam seems to have no moral problems at all. The narrator gets carried away by Tam's pleasure, joining in the mood, "the ale was growing better" and "the minutes winged their way wi' pleasure." But the expression of any powerfully emotional or sexual subject sends him off into emotion-distancing disgressions. The phrase "Bonnie lasses" (l. 16) started a solemn moral disgression. "Life victorious" starts the narrator on a different means of distancing himself from the emotion, the escape into tired neoclassical poetic diction. Here he utters sentimental similes in the diction of the worst contemporary English poetry: "But pleasures are like poppies spread, / You seize the flower, its bloom is shed" (ll. 59–60).

Tam rides toward home through the forest. The weather is fierce, "The wind blew as 'twad blawn its last," and the signs are ominous: "That night, a child might understand, / The Deil had business on his hand" (ll. 77–78). Tam alternately "crooning o'er some old Scots son-

net" and "glowring round wi' prudent cares, / Lest bogles [goblins]
catch him unawares," suddenly comes upon a witches' dance:

> When, glimmering thro' the groaning trees,
> *Kirk-Alloway* seem'd in a bleeze;   *blaze*
> Thro' ilka bore the beams were glancing;   *crevice*
> And loud resounded mirth and dancing.
>   (ll. 101–4)

The word "dancing" provokes the speaker to make a series of moral
generalizations: "inspiring bold *John Barleycorn*! / What dangers thou
canst make us scorn!" He uses chauvinism to distance himself, describing the witches' dance as "nae cotillion brent new from *France*." And
he tries to insure himself from pleasure by invoking class snobbery
when he laments Tam's interest in the witches who are wearing cheap
underwear, "Their sarks . . . o'creeshie flannen."

Although he tries to follow the demands of decorum by keeping his
poem proper, the narrator slips into his natural peasant style by describing the witches' sweat and smells, stopping himself just in time,
so that the poem will have no frontal nudity:

They reel'd, they set, they cross'd, they
    cleekit,
Till ilka carlin swat and reekit,   *every witch sweated and smelled*
And coost her duddies to the wark,   *tossed; rags; works*
And linket at it in her sark!   *danced; undershirt*
                              (ll. 147–50)

The word "sark" sets the speaker off into an especially confused
moral lecture. His *"Tam, O Tam"* admonishes Tam for his interest,
because the witches are not "plump and strapping in their teens," because they are wearing cheap underwear, and because they are:

> Wither'd beldams, auld and droll,
> Rigwoodie hags wad spean a foal,   *coarse; spawn*
> Lowping and flinging on a crummock.   *looping; crook*

His propriety, sense of decorum, concern for money, and Scottish realism merge into a flat statement of gastronomical revulsion: "I wonder
didna turn thy stomach" (ll. 159–62).

But it turns out that a beautiful young witch is present after all. The speaker is mostly taken with her "cutty sark," her short under-shirt, which is "sorely scant." And following the rules of poetry, in true epic fashion he gives its history, its price, and its moral implications.[38] She had worn it "while a lassie . . . in longitude." And its moral significance is that:

> Ah! little kend thy reverend grannie,   *knew*
> That sark she coft for her wee Nannie,   *bought*
> Wi' two pund Scots, ('twas a' her riches),
> Wad ever grac'd a dance of witches!
> (ll. 175–78)

Then he can go no further: "But here my Muse her wing maun cour [fold]; ; Sic flights are far beyond her pow'r" (ll. 179–80). The speaker is constrained by the limits of his poetic power. It is an old epic device to complain about the muse's failure to inspire. But here Burns used the device both to demonstrate his speaker's preposterous use of inappropriate techniques just when the action is getting intense and also, more subtly, to shift the focus of the poem to the events themselves and their affect.

Burns combined, in this digression, a wide range of sensuous imagery and poetic devices to convey the energy of musical and sexual pleasure. Tam is like "ane bewitch'd" watching how his Nannie "lap and flang." And: "Even Satan glower'd and fidg'd fu' fain, / And hotch'd and blew wi' might and main (ll. 185–86). Burns exploits the richness of Scottish diction with "glower'd," which carries the sense of staring both intently and with excitement; "fidg'd fu' fain," which has the sense of the kind of twitching, restless movement that implies sexual arousal; "hotch'd," which connotes erratic, uneasy, jerky movements; and "blew" which denotes rapid, excited breathing. Even Satan is in a frenzy of sexual desire. At this moment, comic and sensual, the emotions take over completely:

> *Tam* tint his reason a' tegither.   *lost; altogether*
> And roars out, 'Weel done, Cutty-sark!'

And Burns uses the device of the rhyming couplet to convey an immediate change in action, as if it occurs as quickly as the rhyme:

And in an instant all was dark:
And scarcely had he Maggie rallied,
When out the hellish legion sallied.
(ll. 188–92)

All is dark. The light of their dancing that lit up the forest is out. The party is over, concluded by Tam's loss of reason.

The sexual evocation changes to fear as the witches pursue the terrified Tam. And at this moment the speaker must pause to give us the epic simile that the rules call for. But Burns uses these similes to intensify the reader's emotional response:

As bees bizz out wi' angry fyke,   *commotion*
When plundering herds assail their byke;   *hive*
As open pussie's mortal foes,   *rabbit's*
When, pop! she starts before their nose;
As eager runs the market-crowd,
When 'Catch the thief!' resounds aloud;
So Maggie runs, the witches follow,
Wi' mony an eldritch skreech and hollow.   *unearthly*
(pp. 193–200)

Each simile—the bees angrily protecting the hive, the predators instantly responding to the sight of a rabbit, an entire market crowd in eager pursuit of a thief—expresses an aspect of frightened haste: the adrenalin high that comes from the urgent need for self-protection, the experience of a flash response, and the excitement of a mob chase. These similes are neoclassical failures and sensuous successes.

It is all very funny, especially when the speaker, his muse apparently back in working order, makes a moral apostrophe, an inappropriate (but very earthy) simile, a prophesy, and gets caught up again into identifying with Tam:

Ah, *Tam*! Ah, *Tam*! thou'll get thy fairin!   *just deserts*
In hell they'll roast thee like a herrin!
In vain thy *Kate* awaits thy comin!
Kate soon will be a woefu' woman!
Now, do thy speedy utmost, Meg.
(ll. 201–5)

The speaker accepts the superstition that witches cannot cross a stream. The chase ends with the witch seizing Maggie's tail, as she leaps over the keystone of the bridge: "The carlin claught [grabbed] her by the rump, / And left poor Maggie scarce a stump" (ll. 217–18). The conclusion, the moral that the rules mandate, is ludicrously inappropriate: "Think, ye may buy the joys o'er dear, / Remember Tam o'Shanter's mare" (ll. 223–24). Maggie, the one innocent creature in the poem, is the only one to suffer.

The setting of the poem contributes to the moral chaos. When Tam sets out, he rides into a storm. The setting gets more ominous with the description of the places of an accidental drunken death, a child murder, and a suicide (ll. 91–96). Then the witches' dance appears out of the dark, death-ridden forest like a blazing church.

The ritual of the witches' coven is described with conventional accoutrements of death; traditional offerings made by witches to Satan: the bodies of unchristened children, the gaping face of a recently hanged thief, a garter that had strangled a baby, the knife a son used to cut his father's throat (ll. 131–42). These details parallel the mention of the child murder and suicide of earlier lines (93–96), describing an uncomic world of genuine evil, of acts that are condemned not only by the "douse folk," but are evil by any standard. And the dead babies have further implications. The murdered children in both sections suggest infants killed to conceal illegitimate births. The "span-lang, wee, unchristen'd" children, consigned to hell because of a theological technicality, recall a rigid, unchristian church.

What do we make of it all? The central event, of course, is supernatural. But it could be a drunken hallucination. Does Burns want us to believe it is possible or is he just joking? Burns uses the old device of a single concrete piece of evidence—the stump of Maggie's tail–to tease the superstition into near-reality. Maybe there are witches and covens and Satan worship. Perhaps the Enlightenment has been wrong after all. And maybe it is all imagined. As in "Address to the Deil," Burns seems both to accept and to laugh at superstitious belief. The shifting tone in and out of comedy and the shifting stance of the narrator, who enters into the subject then draws away from it, add to the elusiveness. There is no factual certainty in this world.

There is no certain aesthetic order except in the silly, rule-ridden mind of the speaker. The creation of the poem is itself wrapped in ambiguity as the speaker vainly struggles with outmoded rules and

takes part in the writing of a great poem in spite of himself. The poem
seems best when the speaker is most spontaneous. But Burns's ability
to make the poem good even when the speaker is applying inappropriate rules defies even the popular idea that all art must be "aff-loof."

And there is no sure moral order except in the comically constricted
mind of the speaker. On this issue the structure of the poem becomes
even more subtly complex. The poem is framed by Tam's relationship
to his wife, Kate, the "sulky sullen dame" who is forever giving out
unwanted advice and making doom-ridden prophecies. Tam returns to
her at the end of the poem, in spite of the narrator's gloomy prophecy
that she "soon will be a woefu' woman." At the center of the poem
Tam, the speaker, and the rest of us gladly forget her and her morality
when we see the blaze and dancing in the forest. Most of the images
of death, however, which are mixed in with the "mirth and dancing,"
are related to family ties—children and parents.[39] The bodies of murdered infants remind us that there can be bad consequences if we ignore
the church's sexual prohibitions.

What then is Burns's moral position? Kate, seen alone, could be a
symbolic denunciation of conventional familial morality, like Blake's
"marriage hearse" ("London"). Tam and the dancing witches, taken
alone, could be symbols of the liberated spirit, like Blake's splendid,
fiery tiger. But the images of murder imply hateful sins. And Tam,
who "had been fou [drunk] for weeks," is not a figure of unmixed
admiration. Neither is the beautiful witch, dancing in her underwear.

In the world of experience there is much that is exciting and much
that is frightening. The reader, like the speaker, is drawn into the
excitement that Tam feels in his "victorious" drunkenness, in the marvelous sight of half-naked witches and a sexually aroused Satan. The
scene in the forest is one that suggests desirable release of natural
forces. But it also suggests violence and pointless evil. And Tam's loss
of reason causes trouble, not greater joy. The new ethical system promised us by benevolism and the liberation promised by Blake's "road of
excess" turn out to be elusive.

Blake said, "Sooner murder an infant in its cradle than nurse unacted
desires." The proverb is amusing and in the tradition of satiric exag-
geration. But the early Blake does believe in the untrammeled expression of desire. In "The Tyger," if we separate ourselves from the narrow,
reasoning questioner, we can remain burning brightly with the tiger

in the forest of the night. In Burns's poem we leave the forest, to go home to sullen Kate.

Many of us would, along with Tam and Burns, risk a great deal to see that witches' coven. The poem obviously advocates the joy, excitement, and emotional release that it symbolizes. And the poem rejects the moral strictures of convention, the aesthetic limits of neoclassicism, and the intellectual confidence of the Enlightenment. But in place of them Burns does not uncritically choose Blake's liberation. The poem reminds us that acting on desire can, quite literally, lead us to murder an infant in its cradle. And if we lose our "reason a' thegither" we are in trouble.

In *Love and Liberty* Burns praised and advocated the freedom of the beggars. He observed the limitations of their way of life but ended the poem with "A fig for those by law protected" and with the party still flourishing. In *Tam o'Shanter* we stay to see the party's end and to experience its ambiguous consequences. What Burns touched on in *Love and Liberty* he fully develops here. Impulse can go two ways, joyous and harmful, and we have no way of knowing which it will be in advance. In the brave new world of spontaneity, we are caught between the dangerous, exciting, joyous forest and safe, sulky, sullen Kate.[40]

This poem is the culmination of Burns's career and one of the great works of his age. After the Kilmarnock Edition he gave up the complexity of the epistles and the satires for the range of emotion that the songs allowed. In *Tam o'Shanter* he brought together the themes of much of his earlier work: the pleasures of drink and sex, the difficulties of marriage, the intensity of the moment, the transiency of nature, the rich sensation of concrete experience. He brought together the techniques: the suggestivity of Scottish diction, the ironic use of neoclassical poetic devices, the sensuous imagery, and the multiplicity of voices. And he combined all the techniques and ideas into this complex vision of a comic, hopelessly elusive world.

In this startlingly modern work, Burns has travelled beyond contemporary beliefs to explore both the joys and dangers of freedom. And he has come back with an answer that is as tentative as modern hope. All the promises of truth to be revealed by the Enlightenment and of freedom to be allowed by the overthrow of political, social, and religious restraint prove attractive but elusive. Tam has to go back to Kate. All we can do is bungle on. We still are not sure exactly what

the experience means or even what happened. But we would do it again
if we had the chance:

> Alas! what bitter toil an' straining—
> But truce with peevish, poor complaining!
> Is Fortune's fickle *Luna* waning?
>   E'en let her gang!
> Beneath what light she has remaining,
>   Let's sing our Sang.

Chapter Five

Conclusion

Burns is one of the great poets of the eighteenth century. He is also one of the first to write about modern sensibilities in a modern idiom. Yet he has generally been given far less attention than is his due. He has been misread as a poet and misunderstood as a man.

Nineteenth-century critics condemned Burns for his venereal sins; twentieth-century critics have faulted him for venal ones. The latter accuse Burns of changing his poetry to make it more salable, even though he wrote and collected songs for years without pay. Critics who would readily grant a persona to any other poet, for some reason deny it to Burns. Instead of allowing him credit for the creation of a brilliantly conceived voice in the character of an uneducated farmer, a voice that eloquently expresses his democratic and universalist beliefs, they accuse him of making his "whole life . . . an exercise in role-playing."[1] Obviously his poetry will be the same no matter what is said about his life. But these moral carpings, in addition to obscuring his point of view, also serve to veil the most wonderful part of Burns, the unity of his life and work.

His life and poetry are remarkably of a piece. Undoubtedly this statement can be made about many writers. But Burns is special because, to an unusual degree, the qualities of the man are consistent with the body of his work. Everywhere, in his letters, journals, poems, songs, and in the first-hand reports about him, he emerges as a man of exceptional honesty and warmth. His capacity for friendship and love touches on genius. I do not know of any writer, with the possible exception of Keats, who radiates so much generosity of spirit in both his writing and his life. He had, to be sure, a satiric bent, and he knew how to hate. But the capacity to hate is related to a person's capacity to love, and Burns knew how to love. The warmth expressed in his poems of friendship, the tenderness in his songs to Jean, the readiness in his songs to enter into the minds of people unlike himself, the respect shown throughout his poems for so many ways of life, his capacity for pleasure, his joyous exuberance make him an extraordinary person in his works and in his life.

He was very much a man of his age, of the late eighteenth century and of modern times. He had many of the modern failings—excessive introspection, uncertainty of purpose, wavering beliefs, overemphasis on physical pleasure. But he combined these drawbacks with many of the modern virtues—self-awareness, readiness to take risks, sturdy independence, respect for divergency, unpatronizing sympathy for the oppressed, and love of freedom.

He shared this early modern spirit, in various ways, with some other writers of the late eighteenth century, especially Boswell, Sterne, and Blake. These writers, along with others—Smart, Cowper, Gibbon, Burke, Paine, Wollstonecraft—are most usefully seen as contemporaries, writers who respond to and help define the age's vast conflicts. The late eighteenth century lacks a single great figure, such as Pope or Wordsworth, who gives definition to the period. But it is consistent with this age that no one is in charge, that it all seems to be a chapter out of *Tristram Shandy*.

Burns can best be understood and most fully enjoyed when he is seen as part of this richly diverse period. And the age can best be appreciated if Burns is returned to his rightful place in it, at the center. Burns captures the period's confusion, volatility, and joy. His variations and experiments, especially when seen along with the work by his contemporaries, provide an early indication of the hopes and problems that the world is heading toward. Everyone is beginning to be on his own, to discover what it means to start life anew everyday. Burns, with his superb independence, with his exuberance and pain, with his refusal to fit in anywhere, is perhaps the age's most typical and articulate spokesman.

Notes and References

Chapter One

1. *The Letters of Robert Burns,* ed. G. Ross Roy (Oxford: Clarendon Press, 1985), letter #125. All future references to Burns's letters will be indicated in the text in parentheses with an "R." I have used letter-numbers only, since they refer also to the first edition, ed. J. Delancey Ferguson (1931).

2. John C. Weston, "Robert Burns's Satire," in *The Art of Robert Burns,* ed. R. D. S. Jack and Andrew Noble (London: Vision Press, 1982), 39.

3. Robert T. Fitzhugh, *Robert Burns: The Man and the Poet* (Boston: Houghton Mifflin Co., 1970), 43.

4. Carol McGuirk, *Robert Burns and the Sentimental Era* (Athens: University of Georgia Press, 1985), 29.

5. *Robert Burns Commonplace Book,* ed. David Daiches (Carbondale, Ill.: Southern Illinois University Press, 1965), 16–18. Referred to in the text as "CB."

6. E.g., Allan Ramsay, preface to *Evergreen* (Edinburgh: Thomas Ruddiman, 1724).

7. *The Poems of Robert Fergusson,* ed. with introduction by Matthew P. McDiarmid (Edinburgh and London: William Blackwood & Sons, 1954), 1:143, and David Daiches, "Eighteenth Century Vernacular Poetry," in *Scottish Poetry: A Critical Survey,* ed. James Kinsley (London: Cassell & Co., 1955), 150–84.

8. James A. H. Murray, "Historical Introduction," in *The Dialect of the Southern Counties of Scotland* (London, 1873). Raymond Bentman, "Robert Burns Use of Scottish Diction," in *From Sensibility to Romanticism: Essays Presented to Frederick Pottle,* ed. Frederick W. Hilles and Harold Bloom (New York: Oxford University Press, 1965), 239–58. David Murison, "The Language of Burns," in *Critical Essays on Robert Burns,* ed. Donald A. Low (London: Routledge & Kegan Paul, 1975), 54–69.

9. John Butt, *English Literature in the Mid-Eighteenth Century* (Oxford: Clarendon Press, 1979), 150.

10. McDiarmid, *Robert Fergusson,* 1:118–19.

11. Butt, *English Literature,* 150, says that readers may have seen an element of the burlesque in Ramsay's works but not objected to it.

12. David Daiches, *Robert Burns* (New York: Rinehart & Co., 1950), 17. See also Burns Martin, *Allan Ramsay: A Study of His Life and Works* (Cambridge, Mass.: Harvard University Press, 1931).

13. Kurt Wittig, *The Scottish Tradition in Literature* (Edinburgh: Oliver & Boyd, 1958), 162.

14. Daiches, "Eighteenth Century Vernacular Poetry," 152. The subject is discussed in detail by Mary Ellen Brown, *Burns and Tradition* (London: Macmillan Press, 1984).

15. John Speirs, *The Scots Literary Tradition* (London: Chatto & Windus, 1940), 124–44.

16. McDiarmid, *Robert Fergusson,* 1:128.

17. Allan H. MacLaine, *Robert Fergusson* (New York: Twayne Publishers, 1965), 148.

18. McDiarmid, *Robert Fergusson,* 1:183.

Chapter Two

1. *The Poems and Songs of Robert Burns,* ed. James Kinsley (Oxford: Clarendon Press, 1968). All future references to Burns's poetry will be indicated in the text in parentheses with a "K." In note section this edition will be referred to as Kinsley.

2. For a history of the verse see *The Poetry of Robert Burns,* W. E. Henley and T. F. Henderson (London: Caxton Publishing Co., 1896), 1:336–42; and Kinsley 3:1018–20.

3. E.g., Edward Young, "On Lyric Poetry" (1728) and *Conjectures on Original Composition* (1759); Joseph Warton, *Essay on the Genius and Writing of Pope* (1756, 1782, 1806); William Duff, *An Essay on Original Genius* (1767); Charles Churchill, *The Prophecy of Famine* (1763), ll.35–36, 45–46, 93–96, and *The Candidate,* (1764), 727–28.

4. See W. P. Ker, "The Politics of Burns," in *Collected Essays,* ed. Charles Whibley (London: Macmillan & Co., 1925), 128–46; and "Robert Burns," in *On Modern Literature,* ed. Terence Spencer and James Sutherland (Oxford: Clarendon Press, 1955), 42–61.

5. "The Muse of Satire," *Yale Review* 41 (1951):85. See also Mary Claire Randolph, "The Structural Design of the Formal Verse Satire," *Philological Quarterly* 21 (1942); Northrop Frye, *Anatomy of Criticism* (Princeton: Princeton University Press, 1957), 223; and Alvin Kernan, *The Cankered Muse* (New Haven: Yale University Press, 1959), 21–22.

6. For a summary of the circumstances see Alexander Scott, "The Satires: Underground Poetry," in Low, *Critical Essays,* 92–93.

7. Lines 31–36 are questionable. Kinsley 3:1050–51 thinks it may have been an isolated fragment. The poem works better without it.

8. Kinsley 3:1095.

9. Burns removed lines 61–65, most likely to reduce the inconsistent tone of flippancy and scepticism. In the original stanza Burns had "brisk

bridegroom" instead of "*Young-Guidmen*" and the sexual pun refers to the Devil's ability to make bridegrooms impotent. Scott, "The Satires," 98, says that Burns excluded it to increase sales. Burns is frequently accused by his critics of economic motives for textual changes (e.g., Daiches, *Robert Burns,* 108–9). But Burns was less mercenary than many other writers.

10. Burns altered this passage from one that referred to Jean. Again the critics find a venal motive rather than a critical one (e.g., Kinsley 3:1132, and Scott, "The Satires," 99, who says the alteration was to make Jean a "nonperson"). The more likely reason is that the new passage is more consistent with Burns's theme.

11. McGuirk, *Robert Burns,* 10–11.

12. See Henley and Henderson, *Poetry of Burns,* 4:292–304.

13. McGuirk, 17.

14. There are several important essays on this poem. See in particular, John C. Weston's afterword to his *The Jolly Beggars: A Cantata* (Northampton, Mass.: Gehenna Press, 1963); James Kinsley, "Burns and the Peasantry, 1785," *Proceedings of the British Academy* 60 (1974):1–21. And Thomas Crawford, *Society and the Lyric* (Edinburgh: Scottish Academic Press, 1979), 185–212.

15. John C. Weston, " 'The Jolly Beggars,' " *Studies in Bibliography* 13 (1960):239–47, and Kinsley 3:1151–52 argue for the exclusion of Merry Andrew's Recitative and Song. Thomas Crawford, *Society,* 206, disagrees. I agree with Weston and Kinsley because the sequence is stylistically and thematically inconsistent.

16. The music is printed in Kinsley. I do not know of any recordings of *Love and Liberty* in print.

17. Kinsley 3:1113–18 notes some debts to Goldsmith. But there is no evidence that Burns had read Goldsmith before the composition of "The Cotter's Saturday Night," and the attributions could be to other authors.

18. *Robert Burns: The Critical Heritage,* ed. Donald A. Low (London: Routledge & Kegan Paul, 1974), 73, 77, 121, 125, 164–65.

19. Ibid., 187–88, 208, 253, 303, 310, 326.

20. Henley and Henderson, *Poetry of Burns* 1:361. Crawford, *Burns,* 175, argues convincingly that this practice of allusion was common in the eighteenth century and still is in the twentieth.

21. Daiches, *Robert Burns,* 150–62; Crawford, *Burns,* 174–82; and John D. Baird, "Two Poets of the 1780's: Burns and Cowper," in Low, *Critical Essays* 119–21. Iain Crichton Smith, "The Lyrics of Robert Burns," in Jack and Noble, *Art of Robert Burns,* 22–23, maintains the tireless attack.

22. Quoted in Kinsley 3:1112

23. See Raymond Bentman, "Robert Burns's Use of Scottish Diction," in *From Sensibility to Romanticism* (New York: Oxford University Press, 1965), 239–58.

Chapter Three

1. Low, *Critical Heritage,* 64.
2. Ibid., 62.
3. Ibid., 68, 70, 71.
4. Ibid., 102–3. Riddell met Burns a few years after his first Edinburgh visit, but her description still applies.
5. Quoted in Robert T. Fitzhugh, *Robert Burns: The Man and the Poet* (Boston: Houghton Mifflin, 1970), 129–30.
6. Ibid., 128.
7. *Robert Burns: His Associates and Contemporaries,* ed. Robert T. Fitzhugh (Chapel Hill: University of North Carolina Press, 1943), 32.
8. Low, *Critical Heritage,* 71–78; 80.
9. Ibid., 86–90.
10. Ibid., 91–92. Wordsworth was seventeen at the time.
11. See James Kinsley, "The Music of the Heart," *Renaissance and Modern Studies* 8(1964):25–36. Reprinted in Low, *Critical Essays,* 124–36.
12. Hugh Blair, *Lectures on Rhetoric and Belles-Lettres* (1783), 315–16.
13. Catarina Ericson-Roos, *The Songs of Robert Burns* (Stockholm: University of Uppsala, 1977), 8.
14. Ibid., 131.
15. See Crawford, *Burns,* 17–24, for a defense of "Man was to Mourn" and my commentary on the same poem in "Robert Burns's Declining Fame," *Studies in Romanticism* 11(1972): 213–15.
16. Ericson-Roos, *Songs,* 10–11.
17. Crawford, *Burns,* 267–68.
18. MacColl is on Folkways Records and Redpath is on Philo Records.
19. P. 16.
20. Sir James A. H. Murray, *The Dialect of Southern Counties of Scotland* (London, 1873).
21. G. Ross Roy, in his edition of Burns's letters (1:251), expresses some doubt about the date of this letter and implies that its authenticity is questionable. If the letter should prove to be a forgery, we will have to revise our assessment of Burns's character upward.
22. A modern text, with a history of the publications and other background material, has been edited by James Barke and Sydney Goodsir Smith, with a preface by J. deLancey Ferguson (New York: Capricorn Books, 1965). See also *The Merry Muses of Caledonia,* ed. G. Legman (New Hyde Park, N.Y.: University Books, 1965).
23. Kinsley 3:1284–85. See also Ericson–Roos, *Songs,* 31–32.
24. Daiches, *Robert Burns,* 340. See also David Daiches, "Robert Burns and Jacobite Song," in Low, *Critical Essays,* 137–56.
25. Ericson-Roos, *Songs,* 109.
26. Daiches, *Robert Burns,* 348–49.

27. The song is a patchwork of older songs. Kinsley 3:1454, gives the many sources. They provide an excellent example of Burns's ability to turn dross into great poetry. (e.g., "My Luve's like a red, red rose" comes for "Her cheeks are like the roses").

28. Daiches, *Robert Burns,* 349.

29. Kinsley, 3:1467.

30. Fitzhugh, *Robert Burns: The Man and the Poet,* 305.

31. "Robert Burns, Writer of Songs," in Low, *Critical Essays,* 157–85.

32. Fitzhugh, *Robert Burns: The Man and the Poet,* 415–29.

Chapter Four

1. Thomas Carlyle, *Edinburgh Review* 48 (1829):270–71.

2. Stopford Brooke, *Theology in the English Poets* (London, 1910), 234.

3. *The Use of Poetry and the Use of Criticism* (Cambridge, Mass.: Harvard University Press, 1933), 98.

4. *Literary Criticism: A Short History* (New York: Alfred A. Knopf, 1957), 352.

5. Daiches, *Robert Burns,* 1. John Speirs, "Revaluations (III): Burns," *Scrutiny* 2 (1943):334–47; also *The Scots Literary Tradition,* 124–44.

6. Northrop Frye, "Towards Defining an Age of Sensibility," in *Eighteenth-Century English Literature: Modern Essays in Criticism,* ed. James L. Clifford (New York: Oxford University Press, 1959), 311–18. Marilyn Butler, *Romantics, Rebels, and Reactionaries* (New York: Oxford University Press, 1982), chapters 1 and 2. John Sitter, *Literary Loneliness in Mid-Eighteenth-Century England* (Ithaca: Cornell University Press, 1982). Fredric V. Bogel, *Literature and Insubstantiality* (Princeton: Princeton University Press, 1984).

7. McGuirk, *Robert Burns.* John D. Baird, "Two Poets of the 1780's: Burns and Cowper," in Low, *Critical Essays,* 106–23; K. G. Simpson, "The Impulse of Wit: Sterne and Burns's Letters," and Andrew Noble, "Burns, Blake and Romantic Revolt," both in Jack and Noble, *Art of Robert Burns,* 151–214.

8. *Spectator* 62 (11 May):1711.

9. *Adventurer* 75 (24 July):1753.

10. See William Ferguson, *Scotland: 1689 to the Present* (New York: Praeger, 1968), 249.

11. See David Craig, *Scottish Literature and the Scottish People* (London: Chatto & Windus, 1961), 77.

12. See John Barrell, *The Dark Side of the Landscape* (Cambridge: Cambridge University Press, 1980), 80–82.

13. See Butler, *Romantics,* chapter 1. She says little about Burns but is useful for the background of the arts in this period.

14. *New York Times,* 12 February 1984, 14.

15. See Katharine M. Rogers, *Feminism in Eighteenth-Century England* (Urbana: University of Illinois Press, 1982).

16. Bridget Hill, *Eighteenth-Century Women: An Anthology* (London: George Allen & Unwin, 1984), 10–11.

17. See Crawford, *Burns,* 236–56 for a different approach.

18. See Sitter, *Literary Loneliness,* vol. 2, 13, and Bogel, *Insubstantiality,* chapter 2.

19. *Sex and Sensibility* (Chicago: University of Chicago Press, 1980), 221.

20. Bogel, Ibid., 158.

21. Patricia Meyer Spacks in *The Poetry of Vision* (Cambridge, Mass.: Harvard University Press, 1967) says, "The act of visual perception . . . leads Cowper back to his ideal state of faith and ease" (206). My reading of Cowper is influenced by Spacks's essay, but I do not find her conclusion convincing.

22. On the influence of Locke on both writers, see Kenneth MacLean, *John Locke and English Literature of the Eighteenth Century* (New York: Russell & Russell, 1962).

23. *The Subtler Language* (Baltimore: Johns Hopkins Press, 1959), 184.

24. See Bogel, *Insubstantiality,* 36-38.

25. Burns changed, "Epistle to J.L*****k," l.20, from "The style sae tastie & genteel" to "What gen'rous, manly bosoms feel." The alteration is consistent with his emphasis on feelings rather than principles.

26. George A. Starr, "Only a Boy: Notes on Sentimental Novels," *Genre* 10 (1977):517–18.

27. Maynard Mack, *Alexander Pope: A Life* (New York: W. W. Norton & Co., 1985), 144.

28. Kinsley is not certain, for textual reasons, that all of this poem is by Burns (3:1290–91). And its generality and lack of sensuousness are not typical of the songs Burns wrote during this period. But Burns surely did something to it. The images have a rightness that no other poet and few other folk songs of the period achieved.

29. Andrew Noble, "Burns, Blake, and Romantic Revolt," in Jack and Noble, *Art of Robert Burns,* 191–214, is the only study published recently. Noble gives a survey of previous studies of the two poets.

30. Ibid., 195.

31. Ibid., 198.

32. M. H. Abrams in *The Mirror and the Lamp* (New York: W. W. Norton & Co., 1953), 251, credits Burns with "light-heartedly" giving birth to "Romantic Satanism." I see nothing light-hearted about Burns's comment, in or out of context.

33. The problem of whether the speaker in *Tam o'Shanter* is Burns himself, a fictional character, or a group of voices has generated considerable critical discussion. See Crawford, *Burns,* 220–36; Karl Kroeber, *Romantic Narrative Art* (Madison: University of Wisconsin Press, 1960), 3–11; Richard

Morton, "Narrative Irony in Robert Burns's *Tam o'Shanter*," MLQ 22 (1961):12–20; John C. Weston, "The Narrator of *Tam o'Shanter*," SEL 8 (1968):537–50; and Kinsley, 3:1351–54. My own view is that all fictional narrators are a mixture of the fictional and the autobiographical. It seems to me most productive to concentrate on the speaker's artistic function.

34. Harold Bloom, *The Visionary Company* (New York: Doubleday & Co., 1961), 36.

35. Hazard Adams, "Reading Blake's Lyrics: 'The Tyger,' " TSLL 2 (1960):37.

36. Kurt Wittig, *The Scots Tradition in Literature* (Edinburgh: Oliver & Boyd, 1958), 215.

37. Weston, "Narrator," 545.

38. Two essays on the use of parody in *Tam o'Shanter* are Allan H. MacLaine, "Burns's Use of Parody in *Tam o'Shanter*," *Criticism* 1 (1959):308–16; and M.L. Mackenzie, "A New Dimension for *Tam o'Shanter*," SSL 1 (1963):87–92.

39. Burns cancelled several couplets that satirize doctors, lawyers, and priests. He seems to have limited this passage primarily to moral issues that deal with human relations.

40. McGuirk, *Robert Burns,* 149–61, has influenced me on this poem. But my conclusion is different from hers.

Chapter Five

1. Alan Bold, "Robert Burns: Superscot," in Jack and Noble, *Art of Robert Burns,* 216. See also Daiches, *Robert Burns* 108–9, Scott in Low, *Critical Essays,* 98, and Brooks and Wimsatt, *Literary Criticism,* 352. These are only examples. The view is common in Burns criticism but not universal. Crawford and McGuirk are welcome exceptions.

Selected Bibliography

PRIMARY SOURCES

1. *Poetry*

Poems Chiefly in the Scottish Dialect. Kilmarnock: John Wilson, 1786.

Poems Chiefly in the Scottish Dialect. Edinburgh: William Creech, 1787.

The Scots Musical Museum, by James Johnson. 6 vols. Edinburgh: James Johnson, 1787–1803.

Poems Chiefly in the Scottish Dialect. 2 vols. Edinburgh: William Creech, 1793.

A Choice of Burns's Poems and Songs. Edited by Sydney Goodsir Smith. London: Faber & Faber, 1966.

The Kilmarnock Poems. Edited by Donald A. Low. London: Everyman, 1985. Reprint of the 1786 edition.

The Merry Muses of Caledonia. Edited by James Barke and Sydney Goodsir Smith. New York: Capricorn Books, 1965.

The Poems and Songs of Robert Burns. Edited by James Kinsley. 3 vols. Oxford: Clarendon Press, 1968. The standard edition of Burns works. Includes musical notations and extensive, useful notes.

The Poems and Songs of Robert Burns. Edited by James Kinsley. Oxford: Oxford University Press, 1969. One volume reprint of the Kinsley edition, without the notes.

The Poetical Works of Robert Burns. Edited by Raymond Bentman. Boston: Cambridge Editions, 1974.

The Poetry of Robert Burns. Edited by W. E. Henley and T. F. Henderson. 4 vols. London: Caxton Press, 1896. The standard edition before Kinsley's text. Still very useful.

2. *Letters*

The Letters of Robert Burns. Edited by G. Ross Roy. Oxford: Clarendon Press, 1985. Second edition of *The Letters,* edited by J. DeLancey Ferguson, 1931.

3. *Prose works*

The Prose Works of Robert Burns. Edinburgh: William & Robert Chambers, 1839. Reprinted. New York: AMS Press, 1975. Most of the material has been superseded, but it contains Burns's *Second Commonplace Book* and letters from George Thomson to Burns, material not easily available elsewhere.

Robert Burns Commonplace Book. Edited by David Daiches. Carbondale, Ill.: Centaur Press, 1965.

Robert Burns: His Associates and Contemporaries. Edited by Robert Fitzhugh and DeLancey Ferguson. Chapel Hill: University of North Carolina Press, 1943. Contains the *Journal of the Border Tour* and important contemporary biographical material about Burns.

Robert Burns's Tour of the Borders. Edited by Raymond Lamont Brown. Totowa, N.J.: Rowman & Littlefield, 1972.

Robert Burns's Tours of the Highlands and Stirlingshire. Edited by Raymond Lamont Brown. Ipswich: Boydell Press, 1973.

The Songs of Robert Burns. Edited by James C. Dick with *Annotations of Scottish Songs by Burns* by Davidson Cook. Reprint. Hatboro, Pa.: Folklore Associates, 1962.

SECONDARY SOURCES

1. *Bibliographies*

Egerer, Joel W. *A Bibliography of Robert Burns,* Carbondale, Ill.: Southern Illinois University Press, 1964.

2. *Biographies*

Ferguson, John DeLancey. *Pride and Passion: Robert Burns.* New York: Russell & Russell, 1964. Originally published 1939. An important biography.

Fitzhugh, Robert T. *Robert Burns: The Man and the Poet.* Boston: Houghton Mifflin Co., 1970. The most recent biography. Contains new material.

Snyder, Franklyn Bliss. *The Life of Robert Burns.* New York: Macmillan Co., 1932. Reprint. Hamden, Conn.: Shoe String Press, 1968. Some of the material is outdated, but it is still the best biography of Burns.

3. *Critical Books*

Brown, Mary Ellen. *Burns and Tradition.* London: Macmillan Press, 1984. A survey of the Scottish elements in Burns's work.

Crawford, Thomas. *Burns: A Study of the Poems and Songs.* Stanford: Stanford University Press, 1960. A critical survey of Burns's poems.

Daiches, David. *Robert Burns.* New York: Rinehart & Co., 1950. The best general introduction to Burns. Useful for background and critical analyses.

Ericson-Roos, Catarina. *The Songs of Robert Burns.* Uppsala, Sweden: Acta Universitatis Upsaliensis, 1977. A survey of the songs from the standpoint of the music.

Jack, R. D. S., and Noble, Andrew. *The Art of Robert Burns.* London: Vision Press, 1982. A collection of original and reprinted critical essays.

Keith, Christina. *The Russet Coat: A Study of Burns's Poetry.* London: Robert
    Hale, 1956. Reprint. Brooklyn, N.Y.: Haskell Press, 1970. Book-length
    criticism of the poetry.
Low, Donald A. *Critical Essays on Robert Burns.* Boston: Routledge & Kegan
    Paul, 1975. A collection of original and reprinted critical essays.
————. *Robert Burns: The Critical Heritage.* Boston: Routledge & Kegan Paul,
    1975. Eighteenth- and nineteenth-century essays on Burns.
McGuirk, Carol. *Robert Burns and the Sentimental Era.* Athens: University of
    Georgia Press, 1985. An important study of Burns and the British lit-
    erary tradition.

4. Critical Articles and Parts of Books
Beaty, Frederick L. *Light From Heaven.* DeKalb, Ill.: Northern Illinois Uni-
    versity Press, 1971. "Burns and the Triumph of Empathic Humor" and
    "The Necessity of Marriage," 3–20 and 59–80. Places Burns in a roman-
    tic context.
Bentman, Raymond. "Robert Burns's Use of Scottish Diction." In *From Sen-
    sibility to Romanticism,* edited by Frederick Hilles and Harold Bloom,
    239–58. New York: Oxford University Press, 1965. Review of Burns's
    language.
————. "Robert Burns's Declining Fame." *Studies in Romanticism* 11
    (1972):207–24. Burns and romantic poets.
Kinsley, James. "The Music of the Heart." *Renaissance and Modern Studies* 8
    (1964):25–36. Reprinted in Low, *Critical Essays,* 124–36. Essential for
    understanding Burns's songs.
Muir, Edwin. *Uncollected Scottish Criticism.* Edited by Andrew Noble. Totowa,
    N.J.: Vision and Barnes & Noble, 1982. Contains four essays on Burns.
Murison, David. "The Language of Burns." In Low, *Critical Essays,* 54–69.
Noble, Andrew. "Burns, Blake, and Romantic Revolt." In Jack and Noble,
    191–214. The best essay linking these two poets.
Thornton, Robert D. Introduction to *The Tuneful Flame.* Lawrence: University
    of Kansas Press, 1957. An essay on the music of the songs.
Weston, John. "Robert Burns's Satire." In Jack and Noble, 36–58. On the
    genesis of Burns's satire. A sensitive and moving essay.

5. Background
Bogel, Fredric V. *Literature and Insubstantiality in Later Eighteenth-Century Eng-
    land.* Princeton: Princeton University Press, 1984. Barely mentions
    Burns but gives a context that is helpful in understanding his work.
Butt, John. *English Literature in the Mid-Eighteenth Century.* Oxford: Clarendon
    Press, 1979. Standard literary history of the period.
Camic, Charles. *Experience and Enlightenment.* Chicago: University of Chicago
    Press, 1983. Social background in eighteenth-century Scotland.

Craig, David. *Scottish Literature and the Scottish People.* London: Chatto & Windus, 1961. Social background of Burns's works.

Frye, Northrop. "Toward Defining an Age of Sensibility." In *Eighteenth-Century English Literature: Modern Essays in Criticism,* edited by James L. Clifford, 311–18. New York: Oxford University Press, 1959. A seminal essay on the period.

Gay, Peter. *The Enlightenment: An Interpretation.* New York: Knopf, 1966. Best survey of this important influence on Burns.

Graham, Henry Grey. *The Social Life of Scotland in the Eighteenth Century.* London: Adam & Charles Black, 1950. Useful social details of Burns's life.

Grave, S. A. *The Scottish Philosophy of Common Sense.* Oxford: Clarendon Press, 1960. The Scottish Enlightenment.

Hagstrum, Jean H. *Sex and Sensibility.* Chicago: University of Chicago Press, 1980. Treatment of sexuality in Burns's time.

Kinsley, James, ed. *Scottish Poetry: A Critical Survey.* London: Cassell & Co., 1955. Essays by various hands on Scottish literary history. Essay by Robert Dewar on Burns.

MacQueen, John. *Progress and Poetry: The Enlightenment and Scottish Literature.* Edinburgh: Scottish Academic Press, 1982.

McDiarmid, Matthew P. Introduction to *The Poems of Robert Fergusson.* Edinburgh: William Blackwood & Sons, 1954. The best survey of eighteenth-century Scottish literature.

Price, Martin. *To the Palace of Wisdom.* New York: Doubleday & Co., 1964. An important survey of the period. No mention of Burns.

Sitter, John. *Literary Loneliness in Eighteenth-Century England.* Ithaca: Cornell University Press, 1982. Covers the period just before Burns.

Starr, George. "Only a Boy; Notes on Sentimental Novels." *Genre* 10 (1977):501–27. Benevolism in the novel.

Stone, Lawrence. *The Family, Sex and Marriage in England 1500–1800.* New York: Harper & Row, 1977. Important for the context of Burns's ideas.

Thomas, Keith. *Man and the Natural World.* New York: Pantheon Books, 1983. Useful for its survey of attitudes toward animals.

Wittig, Kurt. *The Scottish Tradition in Literature.* London: Oliver & Boyd, 1958. Examines the specific Scottish elements in Scottish literature from the Middle Ages to the present.

Index

Addison, Joseph, 4, 8, 15, 65, 108
Aiken, Robert, 36, 38
American Revolution, 1, 28, 93, 105, 127
Anstey, Christopher, 39
Aristotle, 107
Armour, Jean, 23–24, 80–83, 90, 100, 139
Ayrshire, 1–2, 123, 125–26

Bacchae, The, 57
Beattie, James, 73
Benevolism, 7–10, 21, 27, 34, 39, 43–44, 45–46, 53, 57, 61, 64, 120–21, 122–23, 129, 136
Bible, 4, 36, 38, 43, 46–48, 60, 79, 119, 126, 127
Blacklock, Thomas, 69
Blair, Hugh, 52, 69, 70, 73, 96–97
Blair, Robert, 59, 74, 113
Blake, William, 60, 61, 104–5, 109, 127–30, 136–37, 140; "London," 128, 136, 146n29; *Marriage of Heaven and Hell, The,* 129, 136; "Tyger, The," 129–30, 136
Bogel Fredric, 113
Bolingbroke, Henry St. John, 8
Boswell, James, 104, 113, 118–20, 122, 126, 140; *London Journal,* 118–19
Brooks, Cleanth, 104
Brown, Richard, 21
Burnes, William (Burns's father), 1–2, 4, 7, 21
Burney, Frances, 111
Burns, Gilbert, 20
Burns, Robert, born in Ayrshire, 1; Critical theories, 26, 67–68, 70–71, 78, 107–9, 127–28; Depression recurs, 3, 92, 99; Dies, 102; dissipation, 2; Edinburgh Edition published in 1787, 71–72; Edinburgh, first visit to, 69–70; Editor of *Scots Musical Museum,* 77; education, 1, 4–5; father, conflict with, 2–3; father dies, 21; Fergusson's influence, 4, 18–19, 21, 22–23, 25, 39–40, 58, 125; Folk songs' influence, 4, 15, 73–74; Health declines, 98–99;

Kilmarnock Edition, published, under title of *Poems Chiefly in the Scottish Dialect,* 20; Knowledge of music, 77; Marries Jean Armour, 81; personality, 3–4, 71, 80; "Ploughman-poet," 70–71; Poetry writing starts, 20; politics, 27–28, 33, 88–93, 97–98, 112, 123–24; Ramsay's influence, 22–23, 25; readings, 20, 21; religion, 5–10; Scottish language, 14–15, 23, 27, 32, 65–66, 70, 80; Scottish literature, influences, 4, 5, 15, 21, 22, 23, 39–40, 52, 57, 68, (*see also* Burns, Fergusson's influence; Burns, folk songs' influence; Burns, Ramsay's influence; Standard Habbie verse form); Tours Highlands and Border country, 72; Turns to songs, 73–74; Urged to write in more genteel style, 72

WORKS:
"Address to the Deil," 35, 44–49, 60, 74, 88, 127, 128–29, 135, 142–43n9, 143n10
"Address to the Unco Guid," 35
"Address to Edinburgh," 72
"Ae Fond Kiss," 78
"Afton Water," 78, 84, 125
"Auld Farmer's New-year-morning Salutation to his Auld Mare, Maggie," 62, 64–68
"Auld Lang Syne," 126–27, 146n28
"Ay waukin O," 96
"Banks o' Doon, The," 78
"Bessy and her spinning wheel," 77, 93–94
"Braes o' Ballochmyle," 125–26
"Ca' the Yowes to the knowes," 84
"Clarinda," 82–83, 100
"Comin thro' the rye," 100
"Cotter's Saturday Night, The," 58–61, 64, 123–24
"Death and Dr. Hornbook," 127
"Death and Dying Words of Poor Mailie, The," 61

"Dedication, A," 35
"Despondency, an Ode," 74–76, 83
"Duncan Gray," (earlier version), 87, 110–11
"Epistle to a Young Friend," 116
"Epistle to Captain William Logan at Park —," 118
"Epistle to Davie, a Brother Poet," 23–25, 29, 34, 74, 115, 117
"Epistle to J.L*****k," 25, 70, 120, 121–22, 146n25
"Epistle to J.R******," 112
"Epitaph on Holy Willie," 35
"For a' that and a' that," 28, 98, 102, 127
"Fornicator, The," 85–87
"Green Grow the Rashes," 9, 78–80, 83, 87
"Halloween," 127
"Holy Fair, The," 35, 39–44, 52, 57, 61
"Holy Tulzie, The," 35
"Holy Willie's Prayer," 35–39, 57, 58, 74, 102, 142n7
"How lang and deary is the night," 102
"I hae a Wife o' my Ain," 78, 93
"I love my Jean," 78, 82–83
"I'll tell you a tale o' a wife," 85
"I'm o'er young to marry yet," 110
"It was a' for our rightfu' king," 91–92
"John Anderson, my Jo," 87–88
Jolly Beggars, The. See Love and Liberty
"Jumpin John," 90–91
Love and Liberty, 52–58, 60, 61, 64, 74, 127, 128, 137, 143n15
"Man was Made to Mourn," 74
"Mary Morrison," 78
"Merry hae I been teethin a heckle," 84, 93, 109
Merry Muses of Caledonia, The, 84–88
"My bony Mary," 92
"My Harry was a Gallant Gay," 75–76, 91
"O Once I lov'd," 78
"O that I had ne'er been Married," 99
"O Whistle, and I'll come to you my lad," 77, 89–90, 109
"Ode for General Washington's Birthday," 102
"Ode to Spring," 85
"On the Death of the Late Lord President Dundas," 28
"Ploughman, The," 110
"Poor Mailie's Elegy," 61–62

"Rantin dog the Daddie o't, The," 86–87, 110
Red, red Rose, A," 77, 96, 102–3, 145n27
"Remorse," 74
"Rights of Woman, The," 112
"Second Epistle to Davie," 115
"Scots Wha Hae," 28, 97–98, 102, 123–24
"Song—," 100
"Tam Glen," 89–90, 109
"Tam o'Shanter," 21, 58, 92, 102, 112, 129–38, 146n33, 147n39
"Taylor fell thro' the bed, The," 110
"To a Haggis," 72
"To a Louse," 50–52, 57, 58, 74
"To a Mouse," 62–64
"To J.S****," 29–34, 74, 115, 118
"To Ruin," 74
"To the Rev. John M'Math," 34–35
"To the Same," 25–29, 116–17
"To the Weaver's gin ye go," 110
"To W.S****n, Ochiltree," 115, 120, 125
"Trogger, The," 112
"Twa Dogs, The," 61
"Wha'll m____w me now," 111–12
"What can a young lassie do wi' an auld man," 110
"When Princes and Prelates," 85
"Whistle o'er the lave o't," 84
"Willie brew'd a peck o' maut," 94–95

Burke, Edmund, 140
Butt, John, 15
Byron, Alfred Lord, 58

Calvin, John, 5–6
Calvinism. *See* Presbyterian Church
"Cherry and the Slae, The," 23
China, 109
Chrystis Kirk of the Grene, 39
Church of Scotland. *See* Presbyterian Church
Churchill, Charles, 39
Cleland, John: *Memoirs of a Woman of Pleasure,* 85
Clarinda. *See* M'Lehose, Agnes Craig
Coleridge, Samuel Taylor, 102
Collins, William, 24, 74, 104, 124; "Ode, *Written in the Beginning of the Year* 1746," 112–13
Cowper, William, 5, 59, 61, 72, 104–5,

108, 109, 113, 119, 122, 124, 140,
    146n21; *The Task, 114–16*
Crabbe, George, 109
Crawford, Thomas, 76–77, 143n20,
    144n15, 146n17
Creech, William, 71
Culloden, Battle of, 11, 91
Cunningham, Alexander, 101

Daiches, David, 16, 95, 98, 104
Davie, Cedric Thorpe, 100
Defoe, Daniel, 111
Deism, 6, 8, 34, 50
Donne, John, 107
Douglas, Gavin, 13
Dryden, John, 4
Dunbar, William, 13
Dunlop, Frances Anna Wallace, 59, 99

Edinburgh Magazine, 69
Elliot, T. S., 104
Enlightenment, The, *5–9,* 12, 22, 34, *44–
    46,* 49, 51, 62, 64, 65, 68, 106, 108,
    113, 127, 135, *137*
Ericson-Roos, Catarina, 76, 77, 95

Ferguson, Adam, 73
Fergusson, Robert, 4, 5, 13, 17, *18–19,*
    20, 21, 22, 25, 69, 125; "Answer *to
    Mr.* J.S.s' Epistle," 19, 23; *Hallow-
    Fair,* 39; *Leith-Races,* 39–40; *Farmer's
    Ingle,* 58
Fielding, Henry, "The Roast Beef of Old
    England," 123
Fisher, William (Holy Willie), 35
Fitzhugh, Robert, 4
French Revolution, 1, 28, 93, 97, 99, 105,
    127

Gay, John, 15–16, 18, 52, 55–56, 61, 107
Gibbon, Edward, 140
"God Save Great *George* our king," 123
Goldsmith, Oliver, 5, 39, 58, 72, 109,
    143n17; "When lovely woman stoops
    to folly," 111
Gray, Thomas, 4, 8, 24, 32, 39, 58, 59,
    72, 74, 104–5, 108, 109, 125–26;
    "Elegy Written in a Country
    Churchyard," 16, 112; "Ode on a
    Distant Prospect of Eton College," 75,
    125–26

Hagstrum, Jean, 113
Hamilton, Gavin, 34, 35, 36, 38
Hamilton of Bangour, William, 17
Hamilton of Gilbertfield, William, 17, 22;
    "Epistle II," 23
Handel, George Frederick, 73
Happy Beggars, The, 52
Hazlitt, William, 58
Henley-Henderson Centennial Edition, 58
Henryson, Robert, 13
Herd, David, *Ancient and Modern Scottish
    Songs, Heroic Ballads, etc.,* 14, 73
Homer, 119
Horace, 107
Hume, David, 8, 65, 69, 70
Hurd, Richard, 73

Jacobitism, 11, 75, 91–92, 124, 126
Jeffrey, Francis, 58
Johnson, James, editor of *The Scots Musical
    Museum,* 77, 86, 100, 101
Johnson, Samuel, 104–5, 113; *Rambler
    #*134, 119; *Rasselas,* 16; "Vanity of
    Human Wishes," 107, 112

Keats, John, 139
Kinsley, James, 40, 43, 77, 89, 98
Knox, John, 11

Lapraik, John, 25, 29
Lloyd, Robert, 39
Locke, John, 5, 8, 20, 70
Longinus, 107
Lyndsay, David, 13

MacColl, Ewan, 77
MacDiarmid, Matthew, 15, 17
Mack, Maynard, 34, 125
Mackenzie, Henry, 5, 8, 20, 21, 70, 71;
    Review of Kilmarnock Edition in the
    Lounger, 70; *Man of Feeling, The,* 70,
    83, 121
MacLaine, Alan, 18
Macpherson, James, 4, 124
McGuirk, Carol, 9, 53
M'Lehose, Agnes Craig (Clarinda), 81–83
Milton, John, 4, 45, 59, 60, 125–26, 129
Murdoch, John, 4

Noble, Andrew, 127, 146n29

Ossian. *See* Macpherson, James

Paine, Thomas, 98, 140
Peblis to the Play, 39
Percy, Thomas, 73
Phillips, Ambrose, 15
Pope, Alexander, 4, 8, 15–16, 20, 21, 24, 30, 34, 39, 40–41, 44, 60, 61, 73, 107, 111, 125–26, 140; "Elegy to the Memory of an Unfortunate Lady," 111; "Eloisa to Abelard," 53; *Essay on Man,* 28, 57, 62, 98, 107, 115, 120; *Guardian 40,* 15–16
Predestination, 5–7, 35–38, 48–49
Presbyterian Church, 2, 5–10, 11, 21, 22, 34–39, 41–43, 44–49, 59, 79, 85, 108, 130

Radcliffe, Ann, 111
Ramsay, Allan, 5, 8, 15, 17, 18, 20, 22, 25, 69, 73, 141n11; *Tea-Table Miscellany,* 14, 15, 76; *Evergreen,* 14; *Patie and Roger,* 16; *The Gentle Shepherd,* 17
Redpath, Jean, 77
Richardson, Samuel, 4–5, 20, 111
Riddell, Maria, 71, 144n4
Ritson, Joseph, 73
Ross, Alexander, 17
Rousseau, Jean-Jacques, 8, 70, 113

Scotland, differences from England, 10–13
Scotland, subject of Burns, 123–26
Scots Musical Museum, The. See Johnson, James
Scott, Sir Walter, 58
Scottish language, 12, 14–15; *see also* Burns, Scottish language
Scottish Literary Revival, 5, 10–19, 21, 22–23; *see also* Burns, Scottish literature, influences
Select Collection of Original Scotish Airs for the Voice, The. See Thomson, George
Shaftesbury, Anthony Ashley Cooper, 8, 70
Shakespeare, William, 4, 20, 76

Shenstone, William, 4, 8, 20, 21, 32, 39, 58, 72, 74
Sillar, David, 23
Skinner, John, 17
Smart, Christopher, 59, 61, 104, 140
Smith, Adam, 5, 8, 20, 21, 65, 70
Smollett, Tobias George, 5, 8, 20, 61
Spacks, Patricia Meyer, 146n21
Speirs, John, 104
Standard Habbie verse form, 23, 25–26, 32, 118
Steele, Sir Richard, 8
Sterne, Laurence, 4, 8, 20, 21, 61, 104–5, 113, 114, 116–23, 140; *Sentimental Journey, A,* 118, 120; *Tristram Shandy,* 116–17, 122, 140
Stewart, Dugald, 69
Stuart, Prince Charles, 11, 91
Swift, Jonathan, 107

Tarbolton Bachelors' Club, 20
Thomson, George, editor of *The Select Collection of Original Scotish Airs for the Voice,* 77, 100–102
Thomson, James, 8, 20, 21, 32, 58, 61, 123, 124; *Castle of Indolence,* 23; "Rule, Britania," 123; *Seasons, The,* 114, 125

Union, Act of, 11
Universalism, 6, 8, 10, 21, 34, 61

Wallace, Sir William, 13, 97
Warton, Joseph, 108
Wasserman, Earl, 119
Watson, James, 15, 73; *Choice Collection of Comic and Serious Scots Poems,* 14
Weston, John, 3
Wimsatt, W. K., 104
Wollstonecraft, Mary, 106–7, 112, 140
Wordsworth, William, 72, 102, 125–26, 140

Young, Edward, 59, 74, 83, 113